Praise for *The Reward of Knowing*

John Collopy is one of the real estate industry's most influential leaders. He's also one of its most authentic people. John's new book is a brutally honest account of how far he came to rise so high. It's an absolute must for anyone who enjoys stories of grit, resilience, and the courage to move forward no matter what. John is a huge success in business— but sharing his story may be his biggest triumph of all. Read this book!

—Dave Liniger

Chairman and Co-Founder RE/MAX

In The Reward of Knowing, *John Collopy leads you on a journey of self-discovery and awareness that can only be taught by someone who has been there. John opens his heart and soul in this poignant and powerful story of his life and career. Simply said—this book is life changing!*

—Margaret Kelly

Former CEO RE/MAX World Headquarters

John Collopy's life story is like none other. The obstacles he had to overcome in his life made him the genuine, hardworking man he is today. Because of his honesty and knowledge, he has been one of the biggest influences in my career. No matter where you are in life, you can always benefit from John's message of being truthful to yourself.

—Brenda Tushaus

COO, RE/MAX Results

John shares his own life story complete with his failures, successes, and mistakes. More importantly, John ties his experiences into why many people fail to achieve the success they desire due to their own internal fears. I can't recall any book that so clearly lays out the connection between talent, drive, and internal demons and how these all relate to the difference between success and failure in life as well as in business. My kudos not just for his willingness to share his life, but how he reveals that even the best have challenges and tragedies in our past. How we deal with our past has the greatest impact on our future and whether we beat our demons or they beat us.

—Steve Murray

President, REAL Trends

The
REWARD
of
KNOWING

The
REWARD
of
KNOWING

JOHN COLLOPY

Advantage.

Published by Advantage, Charleston, South Carolina.
Member of Advantage Media Group.

ADVANTAGE is a registered trademark, and the Advantage colophon is a trademark of Advantage Media Group, Inc.

Printed in the United States of America.

10 9 8 7 6 5 4 3 2 1

ISBN: 978-1-59932-845-4
LCCN: 2017964141

Cover design by Carly Blake.
Layout design by Megan Elger.

This publication is designed to provide accurate and authoritative information in regard to the subject matter covered. It is sold with the understanding that the publisher is not engaged in rendering legal, accounting, or other professional services. If legal advice or other expert assistance is required, the services of a competent professional person should be sought.

Advantage Media Group is proud to be a part of the Tree Neutral® program. Tree Neutral offsets the number of trees consumed in the production and printing of this book by taking proactive steps such as planting trees in direct proportion to the number of trees used to print books. To learn more about Tree Neutral, please visit **www.treeneutral.com**.

Advantage Media Group is a publisher of business, self-improvement, and professional development books and online learning. We help entrepreneurs, business leaders, and professionals share their Stories, Passion, and Knowledge to help others Learn & Grow. Do you have a manuscript or book idea that you would like us to consider for publishing? Please visit **advantagefamily.com** or call **1.866.775.1696**.

Table of Contents

Foreword

I n my career in the real estate industry spanning forty years, thirty-five-plus countries and in every role from salesperson, trainer, recruiter, office manager, franchisor, and even assistant balloon pilot, I have met people from all walks of life, shapes, colors, and ethnicities. This industry seems to be the gathering place for a wide variety of people. Sometimes its circumstances, sometimes it's situational, but for most it's a chance to change their lives. The sad truth is more fail than make it in this business and, as I learned long ago, you don't try real estate; real estate tries you. John's book and teachings will increase your odds of success.

I can say with complete conviction that John Collopy is one of the brightest minds I have ever met in this industry and in my journey in business. Simply, he is extraordinary. Although not Ivy League educated (and I know a few who are), John can run circles around most of them. Perhaps it was the circumstantial challenging journey he took to get himself to where he is today. Faced with what he encountered, most people would have quit. The school of hard knocks will reward you if you stick it out and this has been the case for John. Perhaps it's divine intervention. What is evident, in John's case, is an unwavering conviction and commitment to not quit and the overwhelming sense of obligation he has to the people he leads every day. There is a bit of nastiness and grittiness to John, but there is also a big heart that will extend a hand to someone when they need help most. This is one of his biggest gifts.

John is a fierce competitor who sees the world beyond his home state of Minnesota; he has been a sponge for learning and made his company a showcase of the finest and best practices in the industry. John's biggest reward to himself is not more financial success, but rather how he has changed lives and lifted other people who have struggled like he did in the early years of his life. There are many who have publicly credited John for helping them through their struggles with addiction and abuse.

I have had the pleasure of working with many highly successful people in this industry and have been asked many times what the keys to success are in real estate. It is my belief that this business, in and of itself, is a simple business compared to others. In that context, that is exactly what John Collopy practices every day. He has a clear and simple approach attached to a legendary work ethic. He arrives every day prepared to be a professional. He is very disciplined and keeps a sense of humor connected to an infectious laugh. Essentially, people want to be around him and be led by him. This skill is rare and I believe is somewhat intuitive to John.

John and I have a very special relationship for which I am very grateful. There is great mutual trust between the two of us and, although we occasionally have had some challenges, we have never lost the respect for each other. I think the two of us are, in some ways, kindred spirits, both experiencing difficult journeys that led us to where we are today and a mutual understanding of that journey. I am honored and grateful to call John not just a business partner, but to also call him a friend.

Walter Schneider
Toronto, September 2017

A Word from the Author

In a way, this book sprang out of a conversation I had about five years ago, on our annual family vacation in Maui. My wife, the kids, the grandkids, and I were gathered at a spectacular ocean-front restaurant, enjoying dinner and the sunset. I was talking with my adolescent grandsons and granddaughter, asking them questions and trying to pry answers out of them: How were things at school? Were they encountering the kinds of challenges among their peers that we hear so much about, things like drug use and bullying? What kinds of pressures were they under? What were their friends like?

My grandson asked me why I wanted to know this stuff. I explained I hoped I could be a resource to him and his brother and sister if they ever needed advice, or had concerns they were hesitant to approach their mom with; that I was a nonjudgmental person who'd been on many sides of those kinds of issues in my lifetime. That provoked some skeptical sidelong glances between the kids;

"Yeah, right. What does he know?" was clearly what they were thinking, although they were too polite to say it out loud.

"What do you guys really know about me?" I asked. "I mean, about my background?"

After a little hemming and hawing on their parts, they told me the consensus was, (a) I'm rich, (b) I've always been rich, and (c) my parents were rich, so naturally I couldn't have a clue about the kinds of problems they faced every day. They couldn't have been further off the mark—but I realized that looking at my life from where they were sitting, they'd made a series of assumptions that are most likely shared by everyone I meet. What people see is the guy who's successful in business, who's coaching others to success—someone who has got his life together personally and professionally.

But that's only part of the story.

So I told my grandkids the rest, that although I've been in recovery for years, I am chemically dependent on drugs and alcohol, and that I'd had started drinking in seventh grade. That I'd been a criminal, and I'd been incarcerated. That, far from having been rich all my life, I'd been flat broke, too, and more than once. And that my family, while technically intact, was far from the warm and fuzzy sitcom ideal, thanks to my highly intelligent, brutally dysfunctional dad.

This made an impression, as you might imagine; their jaws practically hit the table. And to my satisfaction, one of my grandsons came to me the next day to confess he was being pushed around at school. What would I do, he wanted to know, if I were in his place? I told him that if I were being bullied, I'd fight, regardless of what the outcome was likely to be. I wouldn't let anybody bully me. I'm not saying that was the right answer, but that was my answer, and he thanked me for being honest.

Being honest is what this book is about.

I'm going to be honest about myself; I hope I'll be able to inspire you to be honest with yourself, too, to separate the "you" that people see and react to, from the *real* you, the person inside who's the sum of your experiences, good and bad, and who dictates your life choices for better or worse. I'm not suggesting I have it all figured out; I'm still evolving, and I intend to keep growing until I die. But I'm in a better place now than I was ten years ago—and the guy I was twenty or thirty years ago wouldn't recognize me at all.

> *Being honest is what this book is about. I'm going to be honest about myself; I hope I'll be able to inspire you to be honest with yourself, too.*

I've had the same therapist, Dr. Mark, for more than twenty years. We talk about the things that get in the way of happiness and being more satisfied with the decisions I make. I told him that I'd started putting the facts of my life on paper—but seeing some of them in black and white was frankly jarring to me, even years after they'd happened. Could I really do this? Should I?

Dr. Mark pointed out that any attempt to write down my story was bound to be uncomfortable, because my life had been uncomfortable—but suggested that to try and clean it up for public consumption would be a betrayal of my purpose, and a disservice to my reader. If by being honest I could help someone else deal with his or her issues, then it would be worth the occasional pang of anxiety.

If you're stuck and can't get to the next level, if you know you're capable of more than you're producing, if you find yourself falling back on the same old excuses for the same self-defeating behaviors, if you're hurting yourself and those around you—until you come to grips with what was done to you in your past (and get over whatever shame you may carry about your part in it), you'll never move forward.

This book has an unusual structure, which I've employed because I think it's the best way to illustrate how I got from where I was—mired in chaos and self-destruction—to where I am now— successful in both the business and personal spheres, and a happy man. I'll share my personal stories (fair warning: some of them are pretty graphic and disturbing), as well as the insights I gleaned in coming through those episodes, in alternating chapters. My hope is that this will help you to draw the connecting lines between experience and growth, and maybe provide some clarity around your own journey through life. If you don't know where you've been, how can you know where you're going? Socrates said it best: "The unexamined life is not worth living."

So far, it's been quite a ride and a learning experience.

Chapter One

WHEN "NORMAL" ISN'T

My dad, Raymond John Collopy, was a smart, hardworking engineer, a devout Catholic, a former Marine, and, at times, a violent alcoholic. I have a photo of him in uniform behind my desk that people always mistake for a photo of me; medium height and stocky, with arms like Popeye's, he was amazingly strong. He grew up in Stillwater, Minnesota. His father, my granddad, worked at a prison and also had a drinking problem. Dad went into the Marine Corps in 1941, got out, and went to the University of Minnesota Institute of Technology on the G.I. Bill, where he earned his BS in chemical engineering. He was working as an intern with Honeywell prior to graduation when he met my mother, an executive secretary there, at a New Year's Eve party. After a few New Years' Eve toasts and nine months of dating, they married and started a life.

When my dad was sober, he was a pretty good guy. He'd play cribbage after dinner with my sister and me, or throw the ball around in the backyard. But drunk or sober, he had a temper and he ruled the roost. He liked things squared away; the house had to be clean and neat, and we kids had to be sure to put our bikes and toys away. We all lived by his rules. My mom didn't work and couldn't drive a car, so she was totally dependent on my dad. When she needed to go shopping, he took her. He paid the bills and handled the household finances.

We lived in northeast Minneapolis, a white, largely Catholic, middle-and working-class enclave where diversity didn't exist. Catholicism was a big part of our lives growing up; except when he was in the hospital, Dad never missed Sunday Mass in his life. Missing it wasn't an option for the family, either.

Dad scheduled everything—even the nights that he'd go drinking, which were Wednesday, Friday, and Saturday. Wednesday night was grocery night, and he and my mother would go out drinking after that. Friday night when he'd get home from work, they'd go out drinking. Saturday, he would go to the bakery and run some errands, and stop for few beers at his favorite joint. Often, I would be with him on those Saturday mornings, and I'd get to go to the bar with him. Then we'd go home and my mom and he would go out that night.

On non-drinking nights, we looked pretty normal. On drinking nights, it was something else. Nothing interfered with a scheduled drinking night. Both of my folks would come home drunk and the fighting would start. Sometimes it was about dinner: what was going to be served, and who was going to cook it. It was always something trivial, and it invariably devolved into yelling and shoving. Sometimes my dad would grab my mom's shoulders and shake her; sometimes in the morning, she'd have a black eye, or worse. In between, thanks to the thin walls of our house, I had to listen to them fight over whether or not they were going to have sex, with Mom refusing and Dad insisting. I remember stumbling into their room once as a little kid, frightened by the tumult, my father cursing at me to get out, my mother saying, "Go to bed." I did, and prayed for them to stop. But my Hail Marys didn't help. The drama played out over and over.

This kind of alcohol-fueled domestic chaos wasn't unusual in our neighborhood. My friends all knew that my dad drank, and most of their dads did, too. My dad would come out into the yard drunk sometimes when I was playing football with my friends and want to play with us. It was humiliating, him slipping down and rolling around into the mud. But lots of guys I knew had it far worse that we did: some of their parents made mine look like *Ozzie and Harriet*. One of my friends had the cops at his house every Sunday morning.

My sister seemed somehow to float above it all. Sometimes, she'd try to mediate and calm things down; other times she'd just tell me that everything was fine, when it clearly wasn't. She was good at compartmentalizing the chaos. Not me.

One rule we all followed in the family was that we never talked about any of this. Nobody ever told the truth. You didn't lie, but you never told the truth. If you tried, you were shut right up. That restriction ran deep on both sides. I remember going out for my mother's birthday one year, when my mom was well into her eighties; my sister, her family, my two cousins, and I had taken her to our favorite restaurant, and I was asking her what her dad's ethnic background had been. Was he mostly Norwegian?

Mom said, "Actually, he wasn't your real Grandpa." She went on to tell us quite calmly that Grandma—our grandmother, her mother—was quite the party girl, especially when it came to the guys who worked on the railroad nearby. Grandma fell for one of the guys and they got married. They scooped her kids up, moved to a little town, and started life over, and my uncle, my aunt, and my mom were told, "Never mention your father again." My mom never saw her biological father or even spoke his name, at least to me, until that birthday dinner some seventy years later.

That's just the way it was. Nothing ever got talked about, about how you felt or what had happened. You just sucked it up and went on.

In fourth grade, I had rheumatic fever, so I missed the last couple of months of fourth grade and was sick all summer long. As a result of the boatload of medications I was taking and no exercise, I went back to school in fifth grade as a fat kid. I think that was the beginning of me feeling as though I was a little bit out of step with my peers. My academics in grade school were strong, but my deportment was a problem, since I liked to give a running commentary throughout the day on what the teachers were doing. This was a habit I'd developed in the hospital to avoid the boredom, and the nurses thought I was funny. My teachers mostly didn't.

By the time I was in seventh grade, I was getting into fights and hanging out with a crew of high school guys from the neighborhood—the crazy guys, the bad guys. I loved it. People talk about how bad gang culture is, but being in a gang gives you a tremendous sense of autonomy and authority that an average fifteen-year-old kid doesn't have. You're just a dork, and we weren't dorks. We were nuts. I wanted to be out there with those guys. I had the sense that being a teenager was negative, that going to a high school dance wasn't something an adult wouldn't be caught dead doing. Prom, homecoming—all of that seemed to be for kids. I didn't want to be a kid. I wanted to go from twelve years old to twenty, *now*.

I started getting arrested—mostly small stuff at first, like curfew violations, minor consumption, loitering, and then shoplifting. The night my father and I finally had it out, my sister had to come down to the station and get me out of jail for some minor crime. I was back home and in bed, and my sister and her boyfriend and my cousin and her boyfriend were downstairs. My dad was cursing at me from his room, telling me what a bum, what a loser I was.

I told him where he could go, and what he could do to himself when he got there.

He came flying into the room, and started punching and beating the shit out of me. I decided to fight back, because that's what I did when anybody swung on me. It was a real fistfight, a tumbling-down-the-steps brawl, with all the other family members screaming at us to stop. I was bigger and stronger now, not a powerless little kid anymore—and I held my own. From now on, there were two men in the house—and if he wanted to beat on Mom, he had to get past me first.

I hated my father for being a violent alcoholic—so, naturally, that's exactly what I was becoming.

I'm not a perfect man today—I'm a work in progress, and always will be—but my life is a far cry from what it was back in my crazy days. I've had tremendous success in business: RE/MAX is the largest real estate company in the world, and RE/MAX Results, the brokerage that my partner and I opened more than thirty-one years ago, is one of the biggest brokerages in the system. We also own one of the largest title insurance companies in the Midwest. We have nearly forty office locations in several markets throughout Minnesota and western Wisconsin. At this writing, we have more than one thousand sales executives and we're still growing, with plans to expand to two thousand sales executives in four years. This year, we will sell more than twenty-four thousand houses, and do over $6 billion in volume.

On a personal level, I'm a happily married man with a beautiful, loving wife, and a family made up of four kids from my wife's previous marriage, ten grandchildren, two daughters-in-law, and two sons-in-law. My wife, Suki, and I both have successful businesses that we actually like working in.

> *RE/MAX is the largest real estate company in the world, and RE/MAX Results, the brokerage that my partner and I opened more than thirty-one years ago, is one of the biggest brokerages in the system.*

I experienced the failures of two previous marriages before I got it right; the end of the second marriage was particularly disappointing and sad to me because we'd tried hard to save it, but neither of us could get past the significant emotional problems we brought with us that ultimately sabotaged the marriage. We'd gone into therapy to try and salvage it; when we finally broke up, she left therapy but I continued in it—and that's made all the difference in my life.

Previously, I'd been diagnosed as suffering from depression; I refused to accept that diagnosis, and I refused to even consider medication. When I finally acknowledged that I needed medication, it completely changed the way the world looked to me. Yes, I still had the same problems and issues, but it was like a curtain had been raised and I understood what other people saw when they looked at the world. It was a brighter place than I'd realized before that. I met Suki during this period, and my ability to sustain and grow that relationship was different because I now had a clearer understanding of myself, and a significantly different reaction to life in general. We met at a social event; I pursued her aggressively, but she admitted she was reluctant to enter in a relationship with me because she still had two kids at home and didn't want them to think they came second to anyone. I guess she thought that would put me off—but for me, that was the right answer, and it only raised her in my esteem.

I fell in love with her before she fell in love with me. We became a couple, and started taking to vacations together. We got engaged on Valentines Day, and got married on Valentine's Day seventeen years later. I legally adopted her two daughters from her previous marriage, Diane and Suzanne; their father's relationship with Suki's two sons was more significant, but we're all one big family now, and all the kids are our kids.

Our wedding was in Maui, our favorite place in the world. For the event, I rented twenty-four town homes to house the fifty-two guests, and flew our families, our friends, and four of my top employees there from all over the world to attend. Suki's family came from Korea to attend, and she was over the moon with joy because it was the very first time all of her family had been together. It was amazing, having everyone who really mattered to both of us there in the same place to witness this, the first real wedding either of us had had, and a defining moment in my life. The whole event was like a wonderful dream, so beautiful and meaningful—and months later, neither of us has come down from it yet. We'd both faced significant struggles in our lives, but this time, we were ready.

My heart has always been in the right place—a strong sense of justice has always been there in me—but when you're chemically dependent, you lose who you are when you lapse into your addiction. When I was high or striving to get high, I lost that person for a long time. When I got sober and had the opportunity to rediscover the better person inside, then my life started changing for the better.

It's been an evolutionary process; five years ago I'd probably have been ready for this, but ten years ago, I wouldn't have been—and twenty years ago, I was living on a different planet. As Suki and I were getting to know each other, I was always very straightforward with her about making full disclosure about who I was, and who I'd been. A couple of my old friends who knew me back when (and who are still my best friends and always will be) thought they'd get me in trouble when they showed her a vintage picture of the bunch of us with a foot-high pile of coke on an end table, snorting lines the size of pencils—but she'd already heard my stories of the crazy days, and just shrugged it off. She's not intimidated by me or by my past. In fact, she loves me dearly, amazing but true. And our wedding just made our love greater.

> *My heart has always been in the right place—a strong sense of justice has always been there in me—but when you're chemically dependent, you lose who you are when you lapse into your addiction.*

Our oldest daughter Suzanne recently got married and decided to take her husband's name in addition to keeping mine.

Life is sweet.

I'm going to try and share what I've learned along the way about turning negative experiences into learning moments. I've often found that though life's experiences can often times be both difficult and hurtful, they can also provide the necessary groundwork for change and growth if you're willing to tell yourself the truth, and to keep moving forward.

Chapter Two

WHAT KEEPS YOU FROM SUCCEEDING?

We're told a lot of things in childhood that don't necessarily match up with reality, and I know mine wasn't the only family in which talking honestly was off the table. That kind of thinking gets passed on from generation to generation. My mom and dad thought that was the way to go because that's what their parents had done. My family wasn't able to deal with me because they had no role models for being introspective.

Too often, things that need to be said are allowed to go unspoken—but we receive and internalize the messages nevertheless. And we bring them to work with us.

I work with sales executives every day who want to grow their careers and improve their lives, but who are stymied by the life issues they bring to work with them. Susan's a perfect example: she has worked with me as a sales executive for almost ten years. After a near-bankruptcy, she rebounded and had two years in which she made $150,000. That isn't rock star money, but it's certainly substantial money. She wants to increase her volume this year to approximately $250,000, and she's trying to figure out how she can adjust her business plan to make it happen.

> *Too often, things that need to be said are allowed to go unspoken—but we receive and internalize the messages nevertheless. And we bring them to work with us.*

I told her the problem wasn't her business plan. She knows what to do; she's done it in the past. Her problem is *she's never done it fifty weeks in a row.* Something always happens to derail her efforts; her personal conflicts repeatedly sabotage her success. She doesn't need better sales skills to sell more houses; she just needs to figure out why she won't let herself do it. And she's not unique; so many people tell me about their desires to do this or to be that, yet they can't get out of their own ways.

WHERE DO THE ROADBLOCKS YOU THROW IN FRONT OF YOURSELF COME FROM?

Our biggest roadblocks come from our experiences in childhood and adolescence; nobody graduates from adolescence without experiencing some turmoil and conflict. No matter how smooth your ride might have been, there were times you failed at sports, there were times you failed at academics, there were times you let your parents down. Those experiences form the adult you are, and can hold you back from the achievements you desire. And that holds true no matter what kind of business you're in.

We operate a real estate brokerage with nearly forty offices employing more than 1,200 sale executives. All of my sales executives *know* the three things they must do to sell more houses—prospect, go on appointments, and follow up—so that's not what keeps them from achieving. What keeps them from achieving is that they don't consistently do what they know needs to be done *every day*—and what stops them from following through are the roadblocks inside of them, not the ones in front of them. This doesn't just apply to those of you in real estate or in sales, but to anyone wanting to change behavior or achieve greater success.

WHY AREN'T YOU GOING TO THE NEXT LEVEL?

Why do you hold yourself back? Why are you sabotaging your success? If you know you have to do certain things every day to succeed, yet you don't reliably do them, why not?

Susan has had terrible issues in her life. Her mother gave birth to her when she was just fifteen; her father was in prison. Now, Susan's son is in prison. It's not that she doesn't know how to sell more houses, it's that she's so overwhelmed by the impact of the experiences she's had and they've cut so deeply into her sense of self-worth. I've seen the pattern repeat itself again and again: She hits a certain milestone in working toward success—then a little voice inside of her starts telling her that she's not worthy of going further, that she's not smart enough or good enough to make more that she already does. So, she stops trying when she should keep moving forward. Yes, she knows the three things she needs to do every day—but she just stops doing them, and succeeds in derailing herself.

> *Now, can you have a bad day? Yeah. You can't have a bad week, though. A bad week knocks you back two or three weeks.*

Now, can you have a bad day? Yeah. You can't have a bad week, though. A bad week knocks you back two or three weeks.

If as a real estate sales executive you aren't calling somebody, then you're not going to get an appointment. There just aren't enough people who are going to call you and ask, "Hey, can you sell my house?" And you've still got to follow up, make sure they're ready to sell, and help them to prepare their house for showings. No matter what business you're in, you don't succeed by sitting by the phone, waiting for it to ring.

Most sales executives who are moderate to poor producers suspect there must be something that other people do that they just don't get; they feel that these others have some sort of secret or edge, but they're not quite sure what that is. But it's really no mystery why they lag behind their more-successful colleagues. They simply don't spend their time wisely, doing the kinds of things that will make them more productive.

The vast majority of real estate transactions for the majority of salespeople come from what we refer to as their *sphere group*, people they know personally, and people with whom they've previously done transactions. While we have one guy that works for us who spends $200,000 on billboards in six months, that's highly atypical. Most real estate sale executives develop a database, and they mine the database based upon relationships. We used to call that "relationship-based selling," and I would say that 95 percent of the sales executives who work for me base their business models primarily on relationship-based selling.

Why aren't they achieving?

First, their database isn't big enough; second, they're not making the proper number and types of contacts with their database; or third, they're not the type of people who other people feel comfortable being with. The first two are easily fixed. The third takes more work. Again, while my examples are drawn from the business I'm in, this holds true in any field: you can't count on catching many fish if you're fishing in too small a pond.

ACCOUNTABILITY COMES WITH A PLAN

I've been in the real estate industry for nearly forty years; I both know it and love it. I've sold it, built it, managed it, and helped sales executives to success in the field through coaching, training, and leadership. When I sit down with people who can't understand why they're not doing better at selling, the first thing I say is, "Show me your business plan." We go through their plan together, with me asking questions: "How many contacts have you planned to make this week? And how many have you actually made?"

I don't go looking for people to coach in my company unless we're about to "career adjust" them (otherwise known as firing). If I'm going to career adjust somebody, I typically give that person six months to get back on track. I rarely have to fire anybody, for reasons other than legal or moral issues. Typically, people either work themselves into a job, or out of the job. With most sales executives, when it comes to productivity-related issues, we put together a plan and agree that if they can't follow through on it, they need to do something else, somewhere else.

But the deeper reasons for failure come from their upbringing. Somewhere along the line, they were programmed for mediocrity, and they were not encouraged to achieve. I'll give you an example: After I sobered up, I worked for the government for a while, and after a couple of years I decided to go into real estate. My mom cried when she heard that I quit my government job; to her, the concept of quitting this government job with benefits and going to work in a 100 percent commission job was insanity.

My mom had a transient, Depression-era youth, but this kind of thinking isn't restricted to those who grew up in hard times. RE/MAX Results had a great intern one summer whose father is a corporate guy, and even though the son did brilliantly with us and showed great promise, his dad made him feel as though having a son who sold houses would be an embarrassment to him personally. If he sticks with real estate, this young man will be making as much as his dad does in five years, but if he follows his father into corporate America, he may never achieve that kind of success.

THE MYTH OF SCARCITY

Do you feel that opportunity is limited, that only so many can possibly succeed, and that maybe you're not one of the lucky ones? Or that there's something semi-unsavory about wanting to make money in the first place?

Who told you so?

Clearly that news hasn't reached a lot of the immigrants, many of whom who have risked everything to come to this country, determined to make good. The vast majority of all the new millionaires in

America in the last twenty years are immigrants, and many of these immigrant millionaires come out of the former Soviet bloc. These people get here, and they look around, and marvel—"Look at this wonderful country: Anything you want you can get in America. That stuff they told us back home about the land of opportunity? They weren't kidding."

But Betty, who grew up here in an affluent suburb, went to private schools, and got a college degree, can't find a job, because "they're not really looking for somebody with a major in history." Nobody prepared her for the reality of the workplace, or encouraged her to prepare herself to thrive in it.

COMMITMENT MATTERS

As long as you refuse to fully commit to something, you can kid yourself that you could do better if you wanted to—but you only half-try. Be honest: how much more could you accomplish if you were willing to commit yourself to it without reservation? If fear of failure is what's really behind your lack of commitment, then you need to examine that.

When I was in treatment for drugs and alcohol, my counselor, Dr. Carl Becker, said, "John, I've got to give it to you, you're one of the most amazing losers I've ever met in my life. You have turned being a crazy loser into an art form. Your life is so exciting and insane that I can't believe the stuff you've done. But one other thing I also know is that you're a coward. You're afraid to find out how good you can be, and you've never been willing to put yourself out on the line and compete, based upon your skills and your intelligence. You've always hedged your bet by being high or nuts."

And he was right. I never found out if I could have gone to college. I never found out if I could have stayed on my high school basketball team. Maybe I couldn't have, but I quit, and I rationalized it by telling myself I was too cool to care. It was safer not to commit—and risk discovering my shortcomings.

If you're not performing up to your potential, what's your excuse?

THINK ABOUT IT:

The messages we get from our parents as kids—both spoken and subliminal—inform our world-views, for better or worse. In my family, the norm was a total lack of openness and honesty about things that We Didn't Talk About: alcoholism, family scandals, bad behavior behind closed doors. But there are all kinds of messages we pick up from our parents that are self-defeating and negative and a lot of them are around how we view success. Which of these do you believe?

- "Everything in life is luck—you're born lucky or not, and if not, there's no point in trying."

- "You're not bright/attractive/competent enough to succeed."

- "Only jerks care about money; only jerks get rich."

Examine your assumptions—especially the negative ones that you use to explain the world and your place in it. Are they true, or are they based on someone else's prejudices or negative views? Whose?

Chapter Three

CLOUD NINE

From the first time I got drunk in seventh grade, I was an alcoholic. I was out with a bunch of guys riding around, drinking whiskey and vodka. It wasn't the first time I'd tasted booze, but it was the first time I really got drunk. As that initial rush of heat ran through my body, I finally felt clever, witty, tough—and less alone. This was who I wanted to be, not somebody who was always on the fringe, or didn't quite get it, or wasn't cool enough. This was a game changer. That it was perceived by adults as a bad thing to do—a delinquent act—was just the frosting on the cake for a kid like me, who'd seen the movie *West Side Story* as a promotional film for gang life. I blacked out that night—but when I woke up, I knew I wanted to get drunk again.

The group of guys I hung out with built a little shack out of scrap lumber on a vacant lot with a wood-burning stove. This was our tough-guy retreat, our territory. The shack only lasted a short time until the cops found out about it, but there were a couple of parks and drive-ins we considered our territory. The cops would spot us driving around and would pull us over to check IDs and whether we'd been drinking, so being apprehended for curfew, loitering, or minor consumption/minor possession was a regular thing.

At age sixteen, I found out about drugs—pills and weed. Adults said they were bad for you, but I knew that adults lied. It was the late-1960s and early-1970s, a rebellious time, and I embraced it fully. I knew many people who sold drugs, so supply was never a problem. LSD, downers—everything was available, and I was into it. Pot was so commonplace it didn't even really count. School was an afterthought; academics had always been pretty easy for me, but I stopped pretending to give a damn at this point. I was becoming less and less involved in anything beyond drinking with my friends. By the time I was sixteen, it was likely that I wouldn't be home for Christmas or Thanksgiving.

I couldn't see the point of staying in school, so in eleventh grade, I dropped out of high school and went to work for a car wash, planning to make enough money to buy a car. My dad wanted me back in school, so we cut a deal: he would sign for a car loan if I would go back to high school. I agreed, bought myself a new GTO, and reentered eleventh grade.

My relationship with my dad at this point was chilly at best: I was very independent, and he preferred not having any involvement with me. When I was getting arrested on a regular basis in my teens, his attitude was, "Go ahead and get arrested, but I ain't coming to get you." That meant that if my sister wasn't able to get my mom to come and get me out, I sat in jail.

Dad got tired of it, and finally told me, "I don't want you living in the house anymore." That was fine with me, and I moved out. It just wasn't working for us to be under the same roof. Now that I'd achieved the independence I wanted, the hatred I had for him as an adolescent had died down. I moved out with my drinking and stoner buddies, and concentrated on staying high and partying. Not surprisingly, we managed to get kicked out of our apartment.

Getting evicted from that apartment seemed like a good excuse to hitchhike out to California with a buddy. Oddly enough, when I was out in California I didn't drink much, because it was harder to acquire alcohol than it was to get LSD when you were a homeless bum hitchhiking in California. I was looking for absolutely nothing other than a good time. Would I have liked to figure out a way to stay there? Yeah, probably, because California is cool and I've always liked it. I was just so ill equipped for it.

At one point, we were staying in Berkeley with a guy we'd met hitchhiking. He had been an early experimenter in LSD back in the 1960s when it was legal, and was one of those people that approached drugs not as just a way to get high, but as a way to expand his consciousness and gain self-knowledge. He offered to let us stay with him for a while. He lived in a commune, and we got to sleep in the garage. The garage was actually an old carriage house, and it was pretty cool. The commune was into Indian religion; they were all vegetarians and total hippies. We were there when their spiritual leader, the *Maharishi*, made a stop at their commune. It was as if Jesus had come knocking; they went berserk. This was a little too much for my friend and me; we packed our stuff up and hitchhiked back to Minneapolis. We figured it was time to go back to being rubes from the Midwest.

When I came back, I moved into an apartment above Elsie's Bowling Alley down in northeast Minneapolis, and spent most of my time with my friends, drinking and getting high. I'd started racking up DWIs, so I didn't have access to my car any more, but I managed to get around on my bike or the bus. I was what you'd call a functioning alcoholic; I was going nowhere, but I was surviving and taking care of myself and having a pretty good time. I got a blue-collar job working at the plant my dad operated, although not in his department, and work was really our only regular contact. And so we developed a weird coexistence, because there's still the bond, no matter how angry you get at your parent or how disgusted you may be with your kid.

I remember an incident at work where I hurt my foot really bad with some chemicals, and I couldn't walk for a period of time. My mom gave my dad some stuff for me, and asked him to bring down to where I lived. He came to the door, knocked, and said, "Here's some stuff your mom sent you." I asked, "You want to come in?" He said, "No thanks," and left. He never came into any house I ever lived in when I was drinking and doing drugs.

My drinking buddies and I decided to get a house together. We pooled our money and rented a pretty nice duplex in the suburbs. We weren't exactly anyone's favorite new neighbors.

Two of the guys worked for a company called Minneapolis Casket; one of them was always bringing home odd funeral memorabilia. The huge light-up cross in our picture window, along with the loud music and our beater cars, probably did not add to our popularity.

One night I woke up in my second-floor bedroom; I don't know if it was the heat or the smell of smoke that woke me, but when I opened my door, I saw the flames filling the hallway. The house was on fire. I threw a chair through my window, shattering the glass and frame, and I hung onto the sill to try and let myself down as far as I could before I dropped. I ended up chopping off the ends of my fingers and I shattered my ankle. But as soon as I was on the ground, I went back in, because as far as I knew, my friends were still in there.

The fire department showed up in time to pull me out alive, but I was severely burned. In the ambulance, dying from the burns and the smoke inhalation, I had what they call an out-of-body experience. The EMT was beating on my chest telling me to breathe; it was as though I was looking down at the scene and my own inert body from above. I had to make a decision whether I was going to go forward to whatever was next, or go back to my body and fight this thing through. I decided to go back to my body.

I was in intensive care for three weeks, and hospitalized for months afterward. I had three skin-graft surgeries and had to undergo a number of separate surgeries to repair my ankle, which had been shattered in the fall. Of the three other guys who'd been living in the house with me, one hadn't come home that night, one was drunk and sleeping in his car, and the third died in the fire.

I had serious burns over half of my body; most of my upper body, including my hands, was wrapped in bandages. The nurses would come in twice a day and rip the bandages off, scrub the wounds and put the bandages back on. The pain was excruciating beyond description. There was a bath that burn patients could sit in to get some relief, but I couldn't use it because I was in traction. The doctors put metal in my ankle to reinforce it, but the repair failed so they had to break it again and redo the surgery. My face healed quickly and without a significant amount of scarring, but my upper body is still heavily scarred.

A couple of times I threw people out who'd come to visit me: One group of people I'd grown up with came and tried to convert me to their belief system. I disliked this approach, and asked them to leave, as trying to influence someone as vulnerable as I was at that point seemed immoral to me. Another unwelcome visitor was a friend of my mom's who started sobbing uncontrollably when she saw me. I didn't like the attention. I didn't like the pity.

When I was released, I moved back to my parents' home. I hadn't lived there for years, and now the constraints that had kept me a *functioning* alcoholic—like work—were off. Now I was always available when anyone wanted to go out and get drunk. That was my only source of entertainment after the fire because there really wasn't anything else I could do. I didn't have a driver's license. I had a little bit of money because I was getting some benefits, so I was drunk as often as I could possibly be, and there were no checks and balances. My alcoholism accelerated at such a rapid rate that I was soon banned from some of the bars in Columbia Heights where I grew up, because I had become that guy who was always passed out in a booth. I didn't have anything else going or any direction to my life, other than to recover from the burns, get off crutches, and get drunk. I was, by my own definition, a bum.

During that stage of stupidity, I came home hammered one night and decided to take my old car to go over to a girl's house for a late-night rendezvous. The police officer who arrested me that night was the same officer who had given me my one of my DUIs. He spotted me and pulled me over. I allowed him to handcuff me, but then I changed my mind and beat him up badly enough that I broke his arm. The cops that arrived at that point jumped on me and beat the heck out of me, which I had coming, then hauled me off to jail. Subsequently, I was told that I was hanging on the bars, screaming at them like a lunatic—"I'm gonna kick all your asses!" Not my finest hour, though I don't actually remember it.

I got out of jail the next day and my friends came and picked me up. I was pretty beat up; I had a broken nose and a couple of broken ribs. We were sitting in a Perkins Restaurant in downtown Saint Paul; I just put my head down on the table, feeling pretty bad, and knowing this wasn't just another DWI. That's when I had what they call in AA my *moment of clarity*; I knew without question that my drinking days were finished. I was worn out, in trouble, and just plain done.

Later on when I met with my attorney, he laid it out for me in plain language: "Here's what's going to happen. Number one, you're going to jail. Number two, you're going to treatment. Number three, I'll get you out of the felony. Let me say it again: Jail, treatment, no prison. If you want more than that, go get another effing attorney."

I said, "I will take that deal." This situation and the way the attorney kept me out of big trouble, but made me accountable none-theless, was one of the big turning points in my life.

He was a good attorney, and made a convincing case that I should be shown mercy because I'd been through terrible trauma with the fire and my injuries, which had impaired my judgment and decision-making abilities. It worked, and as he'd foretold, I went to the county jail for sixty days. I remember sitting around the rec room there, listening to a couple of guys talking about what they were going to do when they got out, and thinking what a miserable bunch of losers they were—and then realizing with a jolt that I was one of them.

I was assigned janitor duty. One day, I was doing my mopping in the restrooms when a guy walked in, looked me in the eye, pissed in the middle of the floor, and walked out, just to let me know where

I stood in the hierarchy. I had to clean it up because you certainly don't go to the guards and say, "You know, someone just peed on the floor." About a week later, I got next to him in the gym when we were playing basketball, put my elbow down his throat, and smacked him a few times just to let everybody know who I was. There were things you had to do just to hold your ground, as silly as that probably sounds.

There was a court-mandated family interview scheduled that the whole family had to attend if I was going to be released early into treatment, but my dad flatly refused to go. He'd written me off. Fortunately for me, my sister was able to talk him into coming. That session was run like some sort of family therapy, and I had to share with my mom and dad what really had been going on in my life all these years; how much I'd abused drugs and alcohol, and the criminal activities I'd been involved in. I don't think my dad paid any attention, but my mom was so freaked out that afterward she literally retained none of what I'd said. My sister just hung in there, not passing judgment, hoping I had hit bottom, doing her best to be supportive and keep her family together.

After my jail time, I went into treatment. When I got out, my counselor in the treatment center was adamant about me needing to go to a halfway house for a number of months. He was confident that my approach to sobriety would not work, that I needed more help and support. I shrugged it off, and went back to hanging out with my friends, going to bars—but sticking to Coke. I did that for a number of months, kind of white-knuckling it. The place we most often went was a real pit called the Matador. The upside to these evenings was that I was able to win some money playing pool because I was the only sober person in the bar at midnight so I could fleece some of the drunks out of a little cash. It was absolutely miserable, because as it turned out there were few things that I had less interest in than being with people who were intoxicated. I mean, it was *awful*; the only thing that kept me going out with them as long as I did was my stubborn determination not to let somebody else tell me who my friends ought to be, so I stuck it out it for a while to prove my point, but it just sucked.

And finally, one Friday night when I ordinarily would have been out with my friends watching them get hammered, I said to myself, "You know, I think I'm going to stay home and order a pizza," and that was the end of me hanging out with the guys and watching them getting high. I finally gave myself permission to not be at the bar. Instead, I started staying home, and it was tremendously liberating to make that choice. Looking back, that was the beginning of me starting to act like a sober person. It was the first time I hadn't gone out on a Friday night in a long, long, time—since I was a little kid—and it was wonderful. Gradually, I stopped hanging around with those guys. When there would be parties, I didn't go. I got used to being on my own and more comfortable with my own company.

As I became more confident in my sobriety, I started reconnecting with my friends, but in different circumstances. We'd go to a football game, we'd go out to lunch, we'd go out to dinner, or we'd go to a rock concert. We would do stuff together, but I wouldn't just hang around a bar or go out to some guy's party where there were kegs of beer and drugs.

I've never been tremendously gifted in social situations, which was one of the reasons that alcohol was such a pleasure to me

> *As I became more confident in my sobriety, I started reconnecting with my friends, but in different circumstances.*

the first time I got drunk. I'd never fit well inside my own skin, and alcohol diminished those inhibitions. Now that I'm sober, I am a little bit inhibited. It sounds weird for a salesperson to say, but I did have trouble getting used to being around people. I was twenty-four years old and I had never been on a date. I had never taken somebody to dinner or to a movie; my relations with girls had all been about parties and craziness; I certainly wasn't the kind of kid parents were likely to welcome into their homes. I remember when I had my first real girlfriend and she took me to meet her parents; that had never happened to me and I felt totally out of my depth.

When I first got out of treatment, I went to the standard AA program where there were a lot of meetings, and a lot of socializing. A few years later I came across an AA group that was called an agnostic AA group, because the idea of a higher power wasn't necessarily defined by the term "God." You still had to accept the other tenets of the program—that the world didn't revolve around you, that there was power in belief and that there was power in the group and power in working the program—but it allowed for a somewhat different, more individual interpretation of what that higher power meant to you. Most of the people in the group were fifteen to twenty years older than me. Some of the people who attended had been sentenced to our group because they had told their probation officers, "I don't want to go to AA because I don't believe in God," and the probation officers could tell them, "Well, we have an alternative for you." That was ultimately the downfall of that group, because we had so many people who came to the meetings that didn't want to be at the meetings and weren't honest or participatory about their sobriety. At some point, I just decided I didn't need that anymore and moved on, but I did use that group for many years and it was very important in my life for a period of time.

I've never resumed drinking; and as time has passed, the struggle no longer looms large for me. Staying straight became more a part of life as opposed to a major struggle for me. Having success with sobriety, both in my career and my personal life, has made it much more appealing.

The toughest part in getting sober was facing up to my behavior, and experiencing feelings that I'd never encountered before because I had always self-medicated my way out of them.

My friends from back in the X-rated days have been my best friends for the last forty-five-plus years. I don't have many close friends from sobriety—none that I'd trust with my life like these guys. Most of them have cleaned up their acts; none of them drink or get high the way we used to. When you're well in your sixties, which my friends are, you can't necessarily kick ass and take names anymore.

Chapter Four

THE TRUTH ABOUT ADDICTION

There are all kinds of addictions and all kinds of addicts. All you have to do is to look at the news to realize what an enormous problem it is, not only in this country but in the world. Addictions—whether they're addictions to behavior issues, or to stimulants, or depressants—run rampant. Our culture has arrived at a point at which there's a greater degree of social acceptance of addiction, without realizing how damaging to the individual and detrimental to society that normalization is.

NATURE OR NURTURE?

Part of our ambivalence around condemning addiction is the unanswered question of how much of it is related to chemical imbalance, versus how much of it is learned behavior. Alcoholics Anonymous's position is that addiction springs from a chemical imbalance and that, if you're chemically predisposed to it, you will inevitably become an alcoholic if you drink at all. Like so many areas in which we're trying to distinguish nature from nurture, there will probably never be a definitive answer. More likely, in my view, is that it's a combination of the two.

In my parents' families, especially on my dad's side, they were stereotypically Irish-Catholic, in that there were a lot of chemically dependent people in our family tree. But I can't make a determination of how much of that was based upon some genetic strain specific to the Irish, versus how much of that was based upon the general acceptance of alcohol abuse as a normal thing. I do know that the more you drink, and the younger you start, the more likely you are to become an alcoholic.

I believe my dad was aware he had a drinking problem. But I think, as is true with a lot of people, he chose that as a lifestyle—and even though there were some bumps associated with it, in his mind the good news was better than the bad news. He just couldn't see himself not having the outlet of going down to the bar with his wife and his friends and pounding down some beers. That's pretty fun—you can't say that's not fun. But when you act out or have other behavior issues associated with it, then it's not as much fun. What made him an addict? It might well have been biology, because he certainly was religious, he certainly was conscientious, and he was always a hard worker. He wouldn't have stolen a nickel from another human being. He had a strong moral code. In the old days, you would have referred to him as a standup guy who always held up his end of the deal. But somewhere intertwined in that was anger and alcoholism.

Of course, this was the culture of the 1950s, where you hid your dirty laundry and didn't express anything negative. I always tell the joke that my family never lied about anything—but they never told the truth about anything either. You never discussed how you actually felt, or what something really meant. And if something was bad, you sucked it up and dealt with it. That's how you became respected as a person of substance: by hiding your feelings, sucking it up and getting on with your life. You weren't supposed to show weakness by being emotional or appearing downtrodden or even showing you were moved. You just got to work, got to school, and got over it.

That's who I wanted to be; I wanted to be Mr. Impenetrable. I wanted to be Mr. Tough Guy. You weren't going to get through to me. You weren't going to see any weakness in me. I'd never tell you what I was really thinking; I'd just fight and claw my way through whatever issues come up, but I'd never bare my soul to anybody.

As I said earlier, I knew from my first drink that I had a drinking problem because of the way it made me feel, the fact that I had a blackout the first time I drank, and that I very much wanted to get drunk again; not just to *drink* again, but to get *drunk* again. Those of us who are prone to being chemically dependent will inevitably end up with a substance abuse problem. If you start drinking and smoking pot when you're fourteen years old, then the odds of you becoming chemically dependent are much higher than if you don't have a drink until you're twenty-two years old. Is that psychological, or does it stem from a chemical imbalance? Darned if I know. I'm not that smart. But regardless, it's tough for those who realize they're addicts to get out of the cycle, or even to decide that they want to change badly enough to make the effort it takes to do so.

ADDICTION TAKES MANY FORMS

I have a number of young employees and I'm shocked at how many of these twenty-somethings smoke cigarettes. You can't convince me that everyone doesn't know by now that smoking's bad for you. So, if you know smoking's bad for you and yet you choose to smoke cigarettes, then you're going to get hooked on the feeling that nicotine gives you, and you're going to become an addict.

If you start doing opiates, the chances of getting out from under that without becoming an addict are extremely low. Meth is allegedly among the most powerfully addictive drugs in terms of how quickly it creates dependence and how much physical damage it does along the way. Clearly, some substances are more addictive than others—but for those of us who are addicts, *anything* can be taken to an extreme. You can be addicted to oxycodone, or you can be addicted to Camels. You can be addicted to gaming, or to watching Internet porn. You can be addicted to fast food. Going to play cards at a casino is not in and of itself a bad thing—but spending money at a casino that you need to support your family *is* a bad thing. Stealing money to go play at the casino is a worse thing—but it's just a natural escalation of the compulsion and/or addiction to that particular behavior. That we joke about these things, or chuckle over stories of addicts' outrageous behaviors is part of the problem. Any of these legal addictions are an outlet for stimulation and pleasure that our society allows, because of our affluence and their easy accessibility. We seem to struggle as a society to find more-meaningful or more-constructive ways to enjoy ourselves. Is it harder than it was fifty years ago? I don't know, I wasn't around, but it sure seems to be easier for people today to do things that are self-gratifying and self-destructive. But it's no easier to break an addiction than it used to be.

Food is another common addiction. All you have to do is walk down the street to see how many people are overweight. If you're overweight, then you are not likely to be happy with yourself, so it's going to affect your self-esteem. Depending upon how overweight you are, it is going to affect your health and you're going to have problems with everything from blood pressure to blood sugar. Once you're overweight, the likelihood that you'll exercise is greatly diminished, so the spiral continues.

Many people who are pre-diabetic could control that by changing their diets—yet they choose not to. Food can so easily become a comforter or a reward; I know if I have a really bad day—"Man, I got my ass kicked today"—then I deserve to go to Dairy Queen and have an ice cream. And if I have a really good day, I deserve to go to Dairy Queen. Food is not just a reward, but entertainment, fun, gratification—everything except simply nutrition, which is what it ought to be. And society, again, tacitly endorses and promotes that attitude.

One of the peculiarities about addiction is that most of the time we're doing it to ourselves. Yes, we may be predisposed to be especially susceptible to addiction but, once again, if you don't light up a cigarette, then you're not going to get hooked on cigarettes. If you don't do Oxycontin, then you're not going to end up with an opiate habit. *If you don't do it, then you're not going to end up there.* If you do use those kinds of things, then you have to understand that it's just another form of Russian Roulette. Will you be among the nearly 10 percent that, according to National Institute on Drug Abuse figures, gets caught up in addiction?

WHY IS IT SO HARD TO KICK A HABIT?

This quote from the Narcotics Anonymous Basic Textbook says it all: "Addicts can be analyzed, counseled, reasoned with, prayed over, threatened, beaten or locked up, but they won't stop until they want to stop." That desire to stop is at the root of the conundrum. Oddly enough, some of the new ways of treating chemical dependency use more chemicals in an attempt to help withdraw addicts from the drug or the alcohol that they're hooked on, ostensibly to make it easier for them, whereas the old-school treatment was simply abstinence. But no matter how you approach it, the method is irrelevant unless you begin with a burning desire to quit. Even if you have that desire, it's hard to look at yourself in the mirror and say, "I'm going to quit," and mean it.

I have a friend who is about seventy years old. He was having health problems from his long-term alcohol abuse and, on top of that, his wife was through with him, and was threatening to divorce him; he finally decided to get sober. After he quit he told me, "This is the greatest thing that ever happened to me. I don't know why I didn't do this before. I'm feeling so much better." He went on and on about all the delights of sobriety, and how wonderful it was. I just found out yesterday that he's drinking again. His sobriety didn't even last two years. That's the power of addiction. He will end up divorced and likely dead sooner than he would have; he knows that, yet he can't make it stick. That's what addiction does.

There are nearly 1,200 sales executives and roughly 250 employees at the companies I'm involved with, and at least monthly I have to deal with somebody who's battling addiction. I've put numerous people into treatment, and told others that if they didn't get help, they'd have to leave their jobs. One of them was a successful sales executive with two kids who was what they call a functional alcoholic, meaning that for the most part she could manage her drinking—except when she couldn't. She went over the edge one too many times, and her husband divorced her. I gave her the "three strikes, you're out" speech; it didn't take long for her to burn through that. She went through treatment programs twice, with no success. The third time she relapsed I told her, "You're done. That's it." I told her that since she didn't want to quit drinking, she ought to quit pretending like she wanted to quit drinking and just move downtown: "You're an attractive woman, you can get guys to buy you drinks and just stay drunk because that's what you want to do. But quit going to treatment, because you don't want to quit." She was incarcerated at least five more times after we let her go from the brokerage, living in a halfway house or the workhouse. She'd appeared to have a great life and a comfortable upper-bracket lifestyle, yet she gave it all up for booze. She probably went through treatment programs five times. But I don't think she ever really wanted to stop—and without that, no treatment can work. I've met people who've been through treatment twenty times and still can't stay clean.

While I'm certainly no proponent of legal prohibition (it doesn't work), society's tacit endorsement of social drinking as a harmless vice doesn't make it any easier. If you go to a professional football game, the percentage of the crowd that's intoxicated is huge. Whether that's right or wrong is not for me to say, but that level of acceptance does make it easier for people to get in trouble—and I see the problem getting worse, not better.

Certainly in the neighborhoods that I grew up in, drinking was such a routine part of life that our parents accepted us drinking as teenagers because they drank when they were teenagers. There was a sort of inevitability to it; it was the norm. Do we as a society do much beyond giving lip service toward promoting a healthier life style? I don't think so. And, of course, the addiction damages more people than just the addicts themselves; their families suffer from their behavior too, and the dynamics are toxic in the home, leading to all kinds of behavioral problems—kids acting out the chaos they see at home, in school, and on the streets, for instance. This is perhaps the most devastating occurrence in America.

ADDICTION HURTS MORE PEOPLE THAN JUST THE ADDICT

I've experienced countless people whose lives have been ruined by an addiction to gambling. In one of the businesses that I'm in, the title insurance industry, many of my competitors' key employees have succumbed to a gambling addiction that ended in them stealing money, losing their jobs, being convicted of a felony, and, in some cases, being incarcerated. An addiction is an addiction, whether you do it in a casino or online.

As an employer, I occasionally have to have conversations with employees that I call career adjustments. If their work habits or private lives or addictions are getting in the way of their performance, we either come up with a solution, or they're adjusted out, as was done with the lady who drank her way through her three chances. A number of years ago, one of my guys had a severe gambling problem. He was a recovering alcoholic and had been straight with alcohol for a long time but now he was hooked on casino gambling. His wife called me about it, saying, "We've got a problem. What am I going to do? We don't have any money." I knew her husband pretty well, so he and I sat down, and I asked him, "What's up?"

He pretended not to know what I was talking about. "What do you mean?"

"I hear you need some help with your gambling issues."

"How do you know about that?"

"Everybody knows about it. What do you think, nobody ever sees you at the casino? You need help." I had found out from the accounting department that the IRS was after him, too.

There are many varieties of interactions I have with employees with addiction issues, ranging from, "I can't have you working here. You're too much of a risk. Go away," to the guy I talked about earlier, who I was able to get into a gambling program at a hospital because he wanted to quit. He knew he had a problem. There are some people who have trouble getting to work on Mondays; I'm fairly confident that I know what the attendance issue is about when that happens, but they're not willing to confide in me. When I ask, "Why aren't you ever here on Monday? What's going on?" and they shrug it off, "Nothing," then I ask them, "Do you like to party?" Some people will open up; other people just clam up. Those people wind up getting career adjusted for not showing up for work, when the underlying issue going unaddressed is that they have a drug or drinking problem.

Often I hear about people's issues from one of my office managers, who'll call me to say, "So and so got a DWI," or, "So and so's in jail. Can you talk to him? Can you reach out to him?" I've visited a lot people in jail. Generally at that particular juncture they're sober, and utterly mortified. They're at the very bottom, and honestly they probably wish I wasn't there, that I'd just forget about them and ignore them and let them wallow in their mess, because they may be sober but they're not ready to confront the size and scope of the problem.

Not everyone hits bottom in a way that's so readily evident. One of the sales executives that worked with me was making seven figures, but he had to hire a driver to take him to home showings because he had so many DWIs. He was still enormously successful judging by outward appearances because he was still able to do his job, but eventually he lost his money. His multimillion-dollar house got foreclosed on and he ended up divorced. Fortunately, he did finally get sober—and he has stayed that way for ten-plus years. When his family got torn up, he made the choice to quit. He didn't want his kids to hate him. That was his bottom: That's where he drew the line. The IRS, the gambling, the foreclosures—those he could shrug off. But his kids didn't want to be around him, and that was what motivated him to enter treatment and stick with sobriety. He ended up achieving an amazing turnaround.

> *All the other issues are that are driving you—your inner feelings, your ability to relate, your dissatisfaction with life, your anger—you're still going to have to work on those once you get sober.*

That's not enough for some people to stop. Some people lose everything. I believe that you can quit drinking without help but I don't believe you can get better without help. Now, if you're an alcoholic, giving up drinking helps because you're not wasting money and getting in trouble with the law. But all the other issues are that are driving you—your inner feelings, your ability to relate, your dissatisfaction with life, your anger—you're still going to have to work on those once you get sober. You can't work on anger management when you're drunk. Sobriety is the first step to getting well if you're an addict—but if you're not dealing with your issues once you're sober, then you're not going to get better, and the chances that you'll backslide are greater.

Addiction erases your personality. It takes away the very essence of who you are. If you're a heroin addict, you're not the person you were before you became a heroin addict. There are so many parts of you that disappear: Sometimes it's happiness that disappears. Sometimes it's love. Sometimes it's generosity. Whatever you lose, you are no longer able to participate in the full emotional spectrum of life. The whole reason we're alive is to experience all these different things that life has to offer, and to participate in the continued experience of everything that's around us. That's what makes life so wonderful. But once you stumble into the fog of addiction, life is no longer important. The addiction is more important, and supporting it takes all your energy. You're not likely to be hanging around with solid, positive people if your main goal is to get another fix, so it overwhelms you. Go to a city bar at 8:30 on a Saturday morning, and you'll see the kinds of people I'm talking about. Those aren't the kind of people I want in my life, or that I would guess you'd want in yours. They're trapped. They're in a hole. They're not anything that they ever imagined they would be. They're not who they used to be. They're not who they were when they were nine years old, running around the backyard, and knew the joy in petting a dog. They're stuck in a bar at 8:30 in the morning, trying to get their life together because they felt like hell when they got up, and that's tough.

HOW DO YOU CURE ADDICTION?

First, you have to admit that you have a problem. Then you have to genuinely want to solve the problem. Nobody can do that for you; nobody can push you, prod you, order you, or manipulate you into it. You have to come to those two conclusions yourself, before you have a chance.

One of the fundamental ideas of Alcoholics Anonymous is to live your life a day at a time. But because I always have to approach things somewhat differently, when I decided to get sober, I told myself, "You know what? Give this five years and see if being sober is better than not being sober," because the alternative was easy to go back to. But living sober, my life improved consistently; even though my other psychological problems and marital problems were still with me, my life was measurably far better than it had been when I was drunk. I wasn't a ne'er-do-well. I wasn't at the bottom any more. I was somewhere in the middle, trying to move up—and the middle's better than the bottom. I was engaged in the battle of life and I now had a chance to solve my other problems. Didn't mean they didn't come up; didn't mean I didn't still make bad decisions. But there were fewer bad decisions, and I got enough gratification in how my life was progressing now that I was sober to make it rewarding to stay that way.

I still had self-esteem issues; I still had questions about whether or not I could keep it together. I still wasn't in touch with a lot of feelings—but I was sober. And that meant I had a chance. Drunk, I didn't have any chance. I was down and I was out, I was a bum. Once you're sober, you can allow yourself to begin to dream about life again, the way you did when you were a kid. That doesn't mean that those dreams are going to be easy to achieve, but at least you can look at them and tell yourself, "I've got a shot."

Having a shot is all I want in life. I don't need to be on top. I don't need to be the top dog. I just want to get up in the morning and know that I have a chance to do something good. That's more than enough.

THINK ABOUT IT:

It's no surprise that addiction is rampant, given the degree to which society either winks at it or actively promotes it—and there are so many things to which we can become enslaved, beyond substances.

Most of us fail to recognize (and refuse to acknowledge) our own addictions—which is why that recognition and acknowledgement is the first of AA's 12 steps: "We admitted we were powerless over alcohol—that our lives had become unmanageable."

Below, you'll see an assessment tool that will help you to determine whether your habit rises to the level of addiction. You may not be a drinker—but you might still be hooked on painkillers, pot, porn, gambling, or overeating—and I'd ask you that if you suspect one of these things is a problem for you, that you take this quiz with that habit in mind—and be honest about the results.

ARE YOU AN ALCOHOLIC?

These questions from Alcoholics Anonymous will help you to determine that.

1. Have you ever decided to stop drinking for a week or so, but only lasted for a couple of days?

   O Yes   O No

2. Do you wish people would mind their own business about your drinking—stop telling you what to do?

   O Yes   O No

3. Have you ever switched from one kind of drink to another in the hope that this would keep you from getting drunk?

   O Yes   O No

4. Have you had to have an eye-opener upon awakening during the past year?

    O Yes   O No

5. Do you envy people who can drink without getting into trouble?

    O Yes   O No

6. Have you had problems connected with drinking during the past year?

    O Yes   O No

7. Has your drinking caused trouble at home?

    O Yes   O No

8. Do you ever try to get "extra" drinks at a party because you do not get enough?

    O Yes   O No

9. Do you tell yourself you can stop drinking any time you want to, even though you keep getting drunk when you don't mean to?

    O Yes   O No

10. Have you missed days of work or school because of drinking?

    O Yes   O No

11. Do you have "blackouts"?

    O Yes   O No

12. Have you ever felt that your life would be better if you did not drink?

    O Yes   O No

If you've answered YES to four or more, you have a drinking problem.

Chapter Five

THE ANGER HABIT

I didn't set out to be an angry guy. There are things we absorb in life that become learned behavior—things that become embedded in who we are—even though we didn't aspire to being that way. I learned anger from watching my father. I've never known or been able to discover why my dad was so angry, whether it was something that happened to him in his childhood, or his military experience, or simply frustrations with his adult life. Clearly, his anger was exacerbated by alcohol abuse, but it didn't only erupt when he was drinking. He was capable of flying off the handle because one of us kids answered the phone the wrong way—for instance, if his job called and received no answer from anyone at home, he wouldn't have had to go to work. It then was our fault he had to go to work because we answered the phone when his job called.

You never knew where he was going to come down; if I broke my bicycle, sometimes my dad would help me fix it, and other times he'd yell at me for being a dumb shit for breaking it. Everyone kind of tiptoed around Dad, because you didn't know what kind of mood he was in. When all was well and we were sitting around watching *The Ed Sullivan Show* together, we were as Ozzie and Harriet as any family in the world, but it wasn't always that way, depending on what else was occurring.

Where I grew up, males fighting each other was just the way it was. If somebody did something to you, you either let them keep on doing it to you—bullying you, pushing you, making fun of you—or you made a decision to stand up and fight. I was always encouraged by my dad to stand up for my rights and not to let anybody push me around. I don't find that wrong: If I had a child today that was being bullied, I'd tell them the same thing: Step up. Fight back. Don't let him do it. Is that the right answer? Don't ask me—I'm not an expert. Fighting was culture-based, status-based, and a necessity if you wanted to be a tough guy or a cool guy or hang around with the crazies. I aspired to hang around with the guys that weren't easily pushed around. That doesn't mean we didn't get our asses kicked sometimes, because everybody does when you fight. But we would always stick up for ourselves.

As I moved into seventh and eighth grade, my success ratio in terms of winning fights wasn't that high—but I was the kind of person that didn't quit, and I wasn't particularly fearful after I realized getting beat up wasn't actually all that bad. I might look stupid for a couple days or I may even get teased a little bit, but in the long run, I'd stood up for myself and felt better for having done so. Even if I lost a fight, at least I hadn't run away. For me, shame hurt worse than a beating. I believe this was one of the behaviors that later turned into a benefit.

My buddies and I had territory that we protected. If you came into "our" drive-in on 49th and Central, you better behave yourself. Showing you weren't afraid gave you status. Even the straight people, the jocks and the academics, all knew who the crazies were and kept a respectful distance. There wasn't much thought about what we were going to do with our lives. I can count on my thumbs how many people out of a very large number of guys that I hung out with had any aspirations to attend college. It just wasn't the role model in the community that we came from. We were just trying to live day to day and get some cheap thrills, knowing there would be some sort of blue-collar work experience waiting for us down the line. We saw ourselves as the cool guys—the street scrappers and brawlers who nobody messed with. Fighting gave us a sense freedom, like we could come and go as we pleased.

It was just how we lived; violence was part of the landscape. If you had to fight somebody after school, there was always a tremendous amount of anxiety that preceded it. Now that I do public speaking, I would equate the feeling of knowing that you're going to fight somebody with the apprehension I feel going on stage—but in both situations, once you're in it, you're in it. Knowing that you had to fight somebody after school was unnerving, but once the tussle started, then you were all in and you either won or you lost. A lot of the time, even a loss would bring some sort of conclusion; sometimes the guy that beat you up would have more respect for you for fighting. When the fights were group against group, they could go on for a long period of time in terms of, "We'll get you next time," not unlike the stuff we hear about with gangs now. The big difference was that since there was limited weaponry, it was much more likely to be fisticuffs than a bat or a handgun.

For the most part, people don't understand the reasons why kids are attracted to gangs. Being in a gang gave me a sense of invincibility; we felt like we could do anything we wanted, any time we wanted to, to whomever we wanted. By the time I was in eighth grade, my gang had largely replaced my family (except for my sister) as a source of emotional support. My parents were just obstructions. My goal was to avoid them as much as possible, to fly under the radar of discipline and lead a crazy life with my friends. I stayed away from home as much as I could.

We were at a party one night in the neighborhood when guys from my high school showed up there. The party was out of their territory, so my friends busted these guys up pretty badly. This was going to cause a problem for me, in that my gang friends didn't go to my school, so I was pretty certainly going to get beaten up on Monday. That seemed like a good reason to carry a gun to school, so I brought one with me. When some guys accosted me in the parking lot about the weekend activities, I pulled the gun and told them to get away from me. They backed off, but said they'd catch me without a gun some day.

A few weeks later, I got into a car accident a half a block from my high school on the Hennepin Avenue Bridge. The guy who was with me bounced off the windshield, smashing it, and I was pretty badly beat up. A kid I vaguely knew from school came running up to the car to see what had happened. I knew the cops were on their way, and I didn't want to risk them finding my gun, so I reached under my front seat and pulled the handgun out. I handed to him, and I told him to go throw it into the river. But he didn't; the idiot took it back to school and told everybody, "Look what I've got in my locker." That didn't go well.

I skipped school for a couple days after the car accident. When I did go back, I was arrested for the handgun and taken to the station in downtown Minneapolis. The cops stuck me in a number of lineups, trying to pin an armed robbery or two on me because I was a dumb sixteen-year-old kid who'd gotten caught with a gun. I'd been apprehended for a lot of low-level criminal activity—loitering, drinking, stuff like that—but it was always my sister who came to bail me out. This was the one time where my dad intervened; I honestly don't know why. Dad called an attorney who was able to get me off because the police had questioned me illegally, since I was a minor and they hadn't brought my parents in as they were supposed to have done. But my problems at school had escalated so much that when the disciplinarian there said, "You're such a pain in the ass. Why don't you just do us all a favor and quit school?" I said, "You know what? You're right. That is really a good idea." That's when I dropped out of school.

When I grew up and went into business, I learned that anger could give me status that I could use as leverage; "You hear what John did? He beat so and so up, the crazy son of a bitch." It intimidated people and made them less likely to challenge me, because nobody really knew how far I'd be willing to go once I got angry. After I sobered up, I wasn't as likely to get involved in bar fights because I didn't get drunk in bars anymore. But I did find having a reputation for being unruly, outlandish, and unpredictably explosive could still be nearly as useful as it was when I was a teenage badass—or at least that's how I perceived it. Plus, it was fun—the adrenaline was a rush, and was addictive in its own way.

I can recall a business meeting where I was going to have to face a guy who my business partner Bill and I were really angry with; when the big shots came to town, Bill told them, "If I was you, I wouldn't have us get in the same room. John's going to do something." Bill knew that I was capable of flying off the handle. But they shrugged it off; "No, we've got to get together and solve this." We got into the meeting, and the guy I was having a problem with insulted me. So, I dove across the table and started pounding on him.

The guy who had called the meeting said to Bill, "Bill, you've got to stop this." But Bill said, "I ain't stopping it. I told you it was going to happen." It was just because I disliked this person so much—and I didn't feel I had the skills or maybe even the intellect to handle this confrontation any other way. Violence had been the go-to outlet for me for so long that my instinct was, "I'll pound him. That will stop this." This didn't improve the situation or enhance our business—but me pounding him in the middle of a meeting made a great anecdote, and added to the "John, he's crazy" mystique.

I very consciously used this as a tool. Physically intimidating people was easy for me; I'm 6'3" and about 215 pounds. That plus my reputation—"I wouldn't say that to him, because he might choke you"—made people apprehensive of me. I remember another meeting with a large group of brokers where I told one guy that if he didn't shut up, I'd shut him up. That was just something you didn't say in a board room. He didn't know what to make of it, but there was another acquaintance of mine sitting next to him who said, "He's not kidding. He's going to drag you out of this room in a minute. So, shut up." I was years away from understanding that this rage was bubbling up from my unresolved feelings about my dad.

Another outlet for my anger was road rage, and the fights it led to. The older I got, the more these roadside confrontations and fistfights became a way for me to prove that I was still tough. I got a kick out of beating up guys who were younger than me. Nobody expected that a guy wearing a suit and driving a Mercedes was going to chase them down, pull over, and fight with them in the middle of the freeway. The first time it happened, I followed a guy home who'd cut me off, and yelled at him from his driveway. That felt good— and my recklessness progressed from there. There was the time on one of the major freeways in the Twin Cities when there was a lane-changing incident; I pulled up alongside the car that had cut me off. There were a couple of young guys in it in leather jackets, trying to look tough. One guy rolled down the window and said, "Fuck you, old man." That took it up a notch—I floored the car, cut them off, then raced ahead and pulled over. They pulled up behind me and the driver got out of his car and came toward me. I jumped out of my car and slammed his head in the car door about four times. He was out. Then the other guy came over and I banged his head off the hood of the car about six times and *he* was out. I got in my car and drove away.

There were more than a handful of those kinds of encounters. Every few months, I'd get in a physical confrontation. There would have to be the right circumstances; I'd have to really be angry. The other person would have to be really angry. The violence level just kept ratcheting up. One night, I was out with my then-fiancée (now my wife) and I didn't like the way some guy drove. I jumped out of my car and tried to drag him out of his car to pound him. When I got back to my car, my fiancée said, "Just so you know? The next time you do that, I'm not going to be in the car when you get back."

That's when I started bringing it up in my therapy sessions with Dr. Mark: "Why am I doing this? What's going on?" It became a major topic in our meetings; why I was so angry, and why there had been literally decades of me lashing out, even though I knew that after the adrenaline rush died down, I wasn't going to feel good about it. It took a while for me to get to that understanding, to accept that it was stupid to put my life at risk for nothing. I wasn't actually winning anything. I wasn't accomplishing anything. I was risking everything. And I was just acting out that same blind rage that I'd grown up with—the rage I finally came to realize I'd learned from my dad.

Learning to dial it down took time. Habits—addictions—are hard to break. I fight my anger addiction every day when my radar picks up that someone is crossing me or treating me disrespectfully, but I try not to get upset about it. We had an incident while we were on vacation recently, and I was very stern with the person in charge about getting the problem solved, but there really wasn't any anger or rage. I've never been rough with the people I work with but if you ask them, the ones who have known me a long time would say that I'm quite a bit different now than I was ten years ago.

The primary life goal for most people is to have some peace, some happiness, and some serenity. When you're angry or disproportionately antagonistic toward somebody, you have to ask yourself, "Does this produce the results I'm looking for, such as peace, serenity, and happiness?" And the answer is a giant NO, it doesn't. You don't feel better afterward. It doesn't help the situation. Yelling produces nothing. Again, you have to ask yourself—does this behavior move me closer to or further from my life goals?

It's hard to consider that in the heat of the moment, but if anger is a problem for you, you need to get in the habit of thinking about that before you act. If I beat up a guy on Highway 169, how does that contribute to accomplishing my goals? Not only does it not contribute, but it's also a high-risk emotional void that I've stumbled into that fills me full of negative energy, and puts me at risk for hurting somebody or being hurt, and winding up on the five o'clock news: "Real estate broker beats up teenager."

But adrenalin is a chemical, and chemical dependency is real. Quitting is hard, but it's possible. We get stuck in these situations all the time where we act like we're powerless—but we're not powerless. We have the faculties to examine and acknowledge that there are alternative behaviors we need to push ourselves to try. Sometimes having a system for that in place is helpful.

Here's mine: When an unfortunate situation or a conflict arises in business, I always use the forty-eight-hour rule: I don't respond to anybody for forty-eight hours when I'm really pissed. I just don't. Even if it means firing off a stern response forty-eight hours later, it's not the same response they'd have gotten from me forty-eight hours earlier. That gives me the time I need to dial down my

> *When an unfortunate situation or a conflict arises in business, I always use the forty-eight-hour rule: I don't respond to anybody for forty-eight hours when I'm really pissed. I just don't.*

response, because the objective is to solve the business problem at hand, and my goal is growth and profitability. So, if I call somebody an asshole, is that going to help my business grow? Probably not. That means I have to find another, more-productive way to communicate.

Anger isn't always played out with fists, and you can fool yourself as I did that somehow it doesn't count if you don't actually hit the person. Because my mother was abused, I told myself I would never do that to a woman. I never struck my first wife, but I yelled at her a lot. At the time, I was so ignorant that I didn't even consider that abuse; "I didn't abuse her. I never hit her." By the time I got into my second marriage I was aware of my outbursts of anger and had dialed that back. But we both had issues with depression that doomed that relationship because I would not consider taking the medication I needed at that point.

I know I'll always be an anger addict in the same sense that I'll always be an alcoholic, even if I never take another drink or get into another fight. I'm more susceptible to a relapse than most people would believe, simply because chemical dependency stays with you. I've just been able to not use today.

I'm lucky that I've had life experiences that reinforce how positive it is being straight, and that I'm able to continue to build a life without losing control or giving in to the anger. I went a number of years without a physical incident—then about two years ago, I did have a have an incident of outlandish road rage. In AA, they would have called that a relapse, but it was so idiotic that it just reaffirmed how stupid that stuff is. Trying to figure out how to communicate and solve problems without being belligerent or throwing my status or weight or rage around to intimidate people is something that I need to be aware of and have to work at every day.

When you've reacted to stress in a violent way for fifty-five years, it's who you are—but we are all capable of dramatic change. It's just really, really hard. There are behavioral issues like this that will be with me until I leave Earth. But the more days in a row that I can maintain peace, the more likely it is that I'll be able to repeat that behavior, just as it's the truth that the more days of sobriety I experience, the more likely it is I can repeat it today—but there's no guarantee. Something traumatic can happen and bring it all back.

I had a number of surgeries a few years ago; I hadn't taken pain medications for a long time, but the surgery was so painful that I took some prescription opiates. I was lying in bed the second or the third day of taking the medication, and I caught myself thinking, "I bet you can find these drugs on the streets just like you used to. This is so nice lying here in bed, high like this. Maybe I should consider it." It was just so crazy that after forty years of sobriety, I could skate so close to the edge so quickly. I realized where I was headed, so I went into the bathroom, flushed the pills away, and that was that.

But the crazy thoughts still come in my mind.

Like my tendency to chemical dependency, my anger will always be in me, looking for a chance to break through my resolve and make a comeback. But I know how to spot it before it takes control, so my chances of keeping it at bay are better than they were, thanks in large part to confronting it in therapy.

Chapter Six

IF YOU'RE NOT IN THERAPY, YOU'RE NUTS

I don't know where I'd be if I hadn't gone into therapy when I did, but I'm pretty sure I wouldn't have the life I have now. There's a tremendous reluctance among people to seek help from a qualified doctor when it comes to emotional issues; I guess the logic is, "Well, I can't be too crazy if I don't need to see a shrink." The fact is, if you can't see how much you need a shrink, then you probably *are* a little crazy.

I've got a sales executive who does every self-help/motivational class/speaker-of-the-month/walk on hot coals type thing out there; you name it, she'll sign on for it. But whenever I meet with her and I ask, "How's it going with your therapist?" the answer always is, "I haven't been going lately." Why is it that she's willing to pour time and money into all of these programs that promise to improve her life or help her to sell more houses, yet she's unwilling to be intro-spective enough to dig into, "Who am I? How did I get here? What do I like about myself? What would I like to change about myself? How can I go about reinforcing the positive parts of who I am, and look for opportunities to grow and improve?"

Things happen to us when we're kids that impact us throughout our lives, things that we haven't accepted or even acknowledged were impactful, but we need to. As I've said, you can't work on yourself until you get sober. But sobriety doesn't fix all the other issues. I've suffered from anxiety, depression, and anger management issues, and while none of these could have been fixed without sobriety as a starting point, it's *only* a starting point.

There's a tremendous amount of power in the 12-step program. There's also a tremendous amount of benefit from going to meetings and having a sponsor. But the sponsor you have in AA is almost certainly not going to be a doctor or be trained in any way to help you beyond what that sponsorship entails. I meet with different sales execu-tives every day, and have for decades. That makes me a tremendous real estate coach, not because I'm the brightest bulb on the face of the earth, and not because I have insights or inspiration from somewhere. It's because *it's what I do* and I've learned from individual behavior.

My therapist meets with four to six people every day and has for decades. That means that when I'm sitting with Dr. Mark, he has a frame of reference for what I'm telling him because he's worked with many people with similar issues. Beyond his education and erudition, his ability to see through to my underlying issues and to help me be honest with myself is a gift, but it's a gift he has worked to hone into a highly professional skill set. Why would anyone not want to work with someone whose life's work is helping them uncover what's holding them back?

YOU HAVE TO KNOW WHO YOU ARE BEFORE YOU CAN DECIDE WHERE YOU'RE GOING

When you listen to Coach Bob or Betty do their shtick at a convention, that will probably provide you with temporary motivation and good feelings, but it's not the same as sitting in a room with one other person who asks you, "Why do you think you did that?" That question forces you to dig into some unexplored parts of yourself for an answer. Sometimes you'll have circle back to that question in six months or six years to find that answer, when you're ready to know. I don't think it's easy to arrive at "why" unless you have a professional guiding you there. Can it be done? Of course, everything can be done. But why would you try to go it alone when there's a whole class of professionals who have dedicated their lives to helping you understand yourself better? Admittedly, it's not easy to find the right person, but keep looking until you do. You'll know when you find the right person; it may not be in the first week or even in the first month, but you'll know, because the light will begin to dawn in your understanding of the events in your life that are driving your behavior.

> *Why would you try to go it alone when there's a whole class of professionals who have dedicated their lives to helping you understand yourself better?*

THERE'S NO QUICK FIX …

Honestly, all this "motivational" stuff is popular because it's easy. It's not real. It's a game. It's showbiz. It's pretty close to BS—not completely, because motivational speakers do offer advice and tips on how to quantify the quality of your life and to put yourself in a system to improve it. So, it's not drivel—it's just not the real thing. It can't answer the essential question of "Why do I do these things?" Walking across hot coals doesn't prove anything; it doesn't provide any meaningful enlightenment. In therapy, you know you've made a genuine breakthrough when you have a moment of clarity, of self-discovery, a breakthrough that provides an insight into a part of yourself you've never previously acknowledged or even been aware of. That's the moment when change "takes," not when everybody in the crowd jumps up and goes, "Yay!" That's all nonsense.

You know when you experience a meaningful breakthrough in therapy because you feel it; you're sitting there as this insight washes over you, and you think, "Oh my. That hurt," or, "Wow, this is really, really difficult." You won't get that clarity parading around a seminar, beating drums, sitting in a sweat lodge, or whatever the flavor of the month happens to be.

My first encounter with anything resembling a therapeutic environment was in that agnostic AA group that I really liked. Nothing could have kept me from going to that weekly meeting. It was an oddball group of people that I had bonded with, inasmuch as I was able to bond with anybody. At the time, I was also dealing with a divorce and we'd been in marriage counseling. The marriage counseling had no positive effect for the relationship, but the counselor had communicated effectively with me. That marriage counselor suggested that I might suffer from clinical depression, a suggestion I rejected. But clearly something wasn't right with me and hadn't been right for many years, so after the marriage counseling broke down, I finally took the plunge into getting therapy. I was reaching out for a different level of help because I could see that I wasn't getting what

I needed any more from AA, and it was time to change direction. I asked my long-time family doctor, "Who do you recommend?" He's the one that sent me to Dr. Mark.

Given my history with drugs, I was frankly uncomfortable with the idea of taking antidepressants. Did it really count as personal progress if you could only do it while medicated? Was it real or fake? But I knew I was not a happy person; there was a consistent lack of joy. When I started seeing Dr. Mark regularly, it was several months in before I finally admitted, "You know, I think I'm depressed." And he said, "No shit. I've been telling you that since we started meeting." To this day, we still chuckle at that; he'd been saying, "You're depressed. You're depressed," and then finally one day I woke up and realized, "Hey—I think I'm depressed."

Since Dr. Mark is a psychologist, he referred me back to my primary caregiver and that's when I went on antidepressants. As anybody has suffered from depression knows, when the medication kicks in and depression leaves, it's like going from gray to sunny. From that moment I really began to improve as that shroud of depression was lifted.

ARE YOUR ISSUES HOLDING YOU BACK?

I see anger manifest itself differently with my sales executives, in that the anger is often more self-directed; they're angry with themselves for their performance. I'm not necessarily able to get close enough to people in business planning to determine if there's violence toward family members or kids, because I'm typically not operating on that level of intimacy, but I do see low self-image, low self-esteem, and a high level of personal dissatisfaction. If I sense that there are issues that are more than behaviorally related to how they're doing business, then I have to refer them to other people. I don't try to be Mr. Know-It-All. I'm just trying to get them to operate a real estate business plan. Over the years, I've worked with a number of sales executives who were suffering varying degrees of personal problems that ultimately ended in them getting divorced. In a sense, the divorces emancipated them, but it emancipated them in a negative way in that the constraints imposed on them by marriage and kids had kept them in check and stopped them from acting on their worst impulses. Once those constraints were gone, they really went off the deep end and their other vices accelerated dramatically to where they could no longer function in their careers. Ultimately, most of them left the business, sinking into chaos or incarceration.

One of the first guys who came to work for our company became more interested in partying than selling. He had been a long-term successful sales person; he was unhappily married, and when he got divorced all he wanted to do was party. The partying led him to a new level of dependency and it introduced him to drugs and alcohol simultaneously. He no longer could perform his job, and lapsed into economic crisis. When you're at the bottom of the barrel, things don't go well. Could this have been prevented if he'd had the guts to go into therapy? Probably.

People don't understand that part of the benefit they can get from therapy is the time it takes to make real progress. In our world, you're going to opt to go to the weekend seminar, because you've been promised that in forty-eight hours, they're going to change your life. *That's a lie.* Nobody's life is getting changed in forty-eight hours. Even with therapy, your life might not get changed in four years—but you'll be moving in the right direction. When I'm coaching people, I like to ask, "Are you better off now than you were a month ago?" If the answer is "yes," then they're winning; it doesn't have to be, "Off the charts better," or, "I am the greatest, I'm killing, I'm a superstar." If they're merely being more consistent in going after their goals, if they're keeping the promises they made to themselves and checking steps off of their to-do list, then they're doing better.

But being coached isn't the same thing as being in therapy. Therapy is a slow, introspective process, and a good therapist won't be telling you what to do, but will guide you toward discovering what it is you really want. The process of therapeutic introspection requires time and consistency, and people have difficulty committing to doing something on a regular basis—even though they know it's what they need.

It's the same thing as exercising on a regular basis; while everyone agrees it's great for you, nobody wants to stick with a schedule. The vast majority of people know that if you go for a daily walk, you're going to be better off than if you don't. The older you get, the more you need to walk. But if you ask them, "Do you walk?" "No." "But you know it's good for you, correct?" "Yes." "But you don't?" "Right." "Why don't you?" "I don't have enough time." "What could be more important than taking care of yourself and living longer?" "Well, I don't know." I think the idea of commitment and consistency are what keeps people from going to go to therapy, or working with a personal trainer, or getting counseling or support. It does have to be an ongoing process, and you have to accept that you won't just wake up on a Wednesday morning and declare, "Hey, I'm fixed."

Can having a coach be beneficial? Of course. In sales, is accountability good? Absolutely. But you're going to find it easier to become accountable to yourself if you first find out who you are. If you have personal problems or issues in your life—a kid who's acting out, or a marriage gone haywire—your coach can't help you with that. You can't perform adequately in your real estate career if you're dragged down by personal problems, because they're going to distract and exhaust you.

If you stick with therapy, you will grow. If you don't stick with it, you'll still get some benefit, but not as much as you would have if you'd stayed with it. There are just so many things that can make people unhappy and irrational that it's hard to move forward—but I do believe everybody can make progress, that unless you have a severe mental health disorder or are a flat-out sociopath, the vast majority of us can profit from very low-level achievements carried out consistently.

People know this, but they still resist. I've thought a lot about what that says about human nature, and honestly, I think it boils down to the fact that people are afraid of the truth. They don't want to know what's going on in the world inside them. Even if they're not comfortable in their skins, they've grown accustomed to living with their problems, and are more afraid of what they'll uncover than they are of living lives constrained by their delusions and fears. So they use the excuse that they can't make time for therapy.

Believe me when I tell you there's absolutely nothing more important you can do—for yourself, for your family, for your work—than making that time to deal with the issues that undermine your happiness and health, and hold you back both personally and professionally.

THINK ABOUT IT:

What you have to do in life is this:

1. Take care of yourself
2. Take care of your spouse
3. Take care of your kids
4. Take care of your spirituality
5. Take care of work

If you don't have the self-knowledge to deal with 1, 2 and 3, then numbers 4 and 5 aren't going to work for you, either.

If you're willing to walk on hot coals, but are frightened of exploring who you are with a therapist, then you probably need a therapist a lot more than you're able to admit. If the point of the hot coal exercise is to free yourself from limiting beliefs or fears, dig a little deeper and find the courage to do the real work.

Chapter Seven

THE WAY UP

Fresh out of rehab, I had nowhere to go except back to my parents' house. My driver's license had not merely been suspended this time but wholly revoked, so I was going to have to prove a significant period of sobriety with back-up from my AA sponsor and present a petition in order to get a new driver's license. I hadn't lived with my parents for a long while, and it was odd to be back. Clearly, I had to get a job and get back out on my own.

I used to walk the five or so blocks from my parents' place to visit my best friend Steve.

Steve ran a big construction crew for a fence company. He was an ironworker and construction guy, and he had an old work pickup truck with the rack and the tools and all that on it. I would borrow his truck to go looking for jobs; I figured I had less chance of getting pulled over in a work truck, so it was a safer vehicle to for me to be driving without a license. I applied for all kinds of jobs, but even though I got the interviews, I didn't get hired.

One morning I came across a listing in the want ads for something called a "community organizer," working for the local branch of a federal government social service agency called a Community Action Agency; I called them and got an interview. The interviewer explained that it involved working with economically disadvantaged people to help make sure they were aware of and signed up for the government programs that were available to them. It was a temporary job, full-time hours, she said, but they only had funding for five months, and it only paid the minimum wage, which at that point was a whopping $2.32. She told me it was mine if I wanted it.

My answer was a less-than-enthusiastic, "I'll think about it."

Because I had no place else to go, after returning his truck, I was still sitting in Steve's living room later that evening when he came home from work. I told him about the interview. "Can you believe these sons of bitches offered me a job for $2.32 an hour? Minimum wage!"

Still in his work clothes, Steve leaned back and surveyed me from the sofa. "How much are you making now?"

"What do you mean?"

"What I said. How much are you making now?"

I shrugged, not sure where this was going. "Well, nothing."

He said, "I don't know, but I'd say $2.32 is a heck of a lot better than nothing."

Hard to argue with that. I said, "Boy, you've got a point," so I called and accepted the job, becoming an official employee of the Anoka County Community Action Agency as a community organizer. I began to get a grasp of government programs and how you build agencies such as that one: by writing grants in order to get funding. I studied the process, and started writing grants and winning them. We got funding for what was called the Weatherization Program, where we could help low-income and senior citizens patch up infiltration on their homes and insulate their attics. And we also got some funding to provide rehab money for low-income and senior citizens. This was during the Jimmy Carter presidency, when the energy crisis was in full swing, and conservation was suddenly a big deal, so money was flowing from the federal government to agencies like ours.

We came up with a way to combine the Weatherization Program with a job training program; we were able to talk the unions into allowing us to hire union guys to supervise crews made up of low-income people who came out of the program as apprentices. By combining all these different funding sources, I was able to develop and orchestrate a pretty amazing program that combined job training with weatherization and housing rehab for low-income folks and seniors.

That was how I tiptoed into the real world, and I was okay at it. I liked what I was doing. Housing, job training, the unions—these were all interesting and worthwhile to me. I was twenty-four years old at this point, and still trying to figure out just what my place in the world might be.

Once I got the job, I bought a house to rehabilitate. You don't have to be a genius to know where wealth is to be made, and that if you're a renter then you're not building wealth. If you're a homeowner, you're building wealth, and if you can fix a house up and resell it, you'll do even better. It was just common sense to me that now that I was straight, I wanted to buy real estate. I wasn't in the real estate business—but I was in the financial common sense business. I did want to get ahead. I put hours into rehabbing that place, all 650 square feet of it, partly because I wanted to spend as little time as possible at my parents' house. I went home to sleep, and that was about it. We kept our interactions to a bare minimum, by unspoken agreement.

> *I wanted to buy real estate. I wasn't in the real estate business— but I was in the financial common sense business.*

I managed to get my little fixer-upper in livable condition and I moved in. This was the period in which I'd quit drinking, but was still hanging out with my old drinking buddies at the bar, sipping Coke while they got hammered. It was a rough transition to make: The fact is, just being sober doesn't make you act like a sober person. It's often said that you need at least a year of sobriety to come down, and this was when I made the choice to change my habits. I stopped hanging around with my buddies. I didn't go to bars. I didn't go to parties. And I started dating a woman I worked with at the Community Action Agency, who was actually the first girlfriend I'd ever had who I went out on dates with. I'd never been out on a dinner date before that. The closest thing I had to a date when I was a teenager is when we'd go to the drive-in movie, but that was also just to get high, and maybe score some fringe benefits. Socially, my development had stopped somewhere in middle school, when I'd replaced it with drinking. Now I discovered that I had a lot of catching up to do.

Later on, as the relationship progressed, this woman wanted me to go down to southern Minnesota and meet her family. I'd never been asked to meet a girl's family. Generally, I was banned from most people's houses because of my reputation in the community, so this was a real first and, frankly, the prospect of meeting her folks was terrifying. She had grown up on a very substantial farm and cattle ranch. I did my poor best to make small talk with her parents, but I was definitely way out of my depth. After dinner, her dad said to me, "Do you want to come take a ride out with me and go look at the herd?"

My response was a very rapid, "No, thanks"; I had no clue that I couldn't have offered him a bigger insult than that. Here the guy wanted to show me his pride and joy, maybe bond a little—and all I could say was "No." I couldn't handle it. I had tremendous anxiety, and for me this kind of social situation ranked close to a near-death experience. I only had one thing on my mind: "*Get me out of here. Get me out of here. Get me out of here. Get me out of here.*"

> *I had tremendous anxiety, and for me this kind of social situation ranked close to a near-death experience.*

I'd moved up the ladder at work thanks to my success in developing and writing new programs, and some other counties now hired me to develop similar programs for them. When I was at the Community Action Agency, the money for those programs had come directly from the federal government. Now the system was changing in that the federal government was going to send the money to the state, and the state was going to administer it, so the state hired me to do that, and to write the rules and regulations. After that, I quit working for the Department of Commerce and went to work for myself as a consultant to agencies doing business with the state under the rules and regulations I'd written.

It was then that I started my first company, called Midwest Solar. We were looking into getting involved in solar collectors (about which I knew almost nothing). I was also traveling as a consultant for both the Commerce Department and the Department of Energy on these energy conservation programs, so I was making a substantial amount of money for someone with my unique history—but it's pretty easy to be an expert when you're the one who set up the first big weatherization program and then wrote the rules for it. Magically, I had become a topic expert in a very small area.

My work involved traveling around Minnesota, but I did not like getting up and driving to Marshall, Minnesota, on a Monday and coming back on a Friday and being "the expert" that had come in to help them. Even though it was lucrative, consulting just wasn't for me. I did like real estate, though, so I decided to get my real estate license and start selling real estate. I wrapped up some contracts that I had to finish with the consulting work, and then went after real estate full-time. I got licensed in 1977 and started selling houses in 1978. For about six months, I was working the equivalent of two jobs before I quit consulting. It was clear that work was becoming the most important thing to me; I had no problem working sixty- or seventy-hour weeks in my twenties. I didn't care. I loved it. Once I got into the real estate business, I got the biggest kick out of it.

About that time, I sold my first little fixer and bought a duplex. My friends were all in the trades, and they'd offer to come over and help me with my fixer-uppers, but most of the time they'd just come over and mess with me, so I got good at doing the work myself. Not all of it—I drew the line at doing the electrical stuff, but I got pretty good at plumbing.

There followed a few years where I was working seven days a week, and it wasn't oppressive or negative because I had no family or relationship pressures (I'd parted company with my former girlfriend at this point). It was just me out selling houses, and I liked it. And I wasn't getting high, so that wasn't getting in the way. I went to work for an old-line Twin Cities real estate company called The Spring Company, which was one of the first companies that Coldwell Banker purchased when they were in the process of becoming the first national real estate company. I became a manager when I was twenty-eight or twenty-nine somewhere between 1980 and 1981, which was crazy young to be a vice president and the branch manager. It didn't generally work that way back then, but my manager, Bill, liked me, so he moved me up despite my youth and relative lack of experience. I was energetic and a workaholic, if you want to use that term; I hesitate to use it because hard work never had any negative consequences on my life. Bill and I liked each other, and he kept promoting me.

I was different; among other things, I was incredibly aggressive. For a real estate manager/broker, there are two parts to the job description, retention and recruiting, and the retention part of the job took me a while to understand and learn, because there's no school to teach you that. That's something you learn on the job. But as for the recruiting part, some people are willing to make phone calls, and some people aren't. Some people are willing to prospect, and some people aren't. I was willing, and Bill knew that. Even though I was unpolished and from a blue-collar part of the Twin Cities, he saw something in my aggressiveness that he thought showed promise. I may not have been academically educated, but I did have a fair amount of common sense, and I was eager and quick to learn. I wasn't afraid to make a mistake, and I wasn't afraid to be told what to do by people that were better at the job than I was. I didn't take offense at direction. Anybody that knew something, I wanted to know it too and was happy to listen.

The first office I managed was in Mounds View. My second was in Columbia Heights, where they built me a new office. I went on to manage the office in Coon Rapids. When I was there, I was working for a different general manager than Bill; this manager, Mike, ended up taking a job running the Coldwell Banker office in Tampa, Florida, and asked me if I was interested in moving down there. By now, I was in my second legitimate relationship, and had been married, so she and I went down to look at the setup in Tampa.

Mike was trying to turn around a company that hadn't been doing very well, and he was eager to recruit me. He promised that I could literally pick out any office I wanted and run it. We drove around checking them out; I really liked the Clearwater office and the proximity to the ocean was really cool. So Wife Number One and I went out and looked at houses, and found a place that we could afford. Mike and I sat down to talk money and what I'd get paid if I moved there, but we were a considerable distance apart on the economics, so my wife and I got back on the plane without having cut a deal.

When I got back to the Twin Cities, I got a call from Bill. He was managing half the Twin Cities by the time, and he said, "I've got a really unique opportunity for you." It was in a very upscale suburb, Minnetonka, right on Lake Minnetonka. Even better, they were inspired to put together a financial compensation program to lure me there that was nothing short of amazing, because this office lost so much money. I had developed something of a reputation for being able to turn bad, unproductive offices into good, profitable offices, which is why Bill offered me this very generous compensation program to move to Minnetonka—and I took it. It was a terrific opportunity.

Not too long after I accepted that opportunity, Mike in Florida called me back to say, "Okay. I got the money, I realigned my budgets, and when can you start?"

I said, "Well, I can't start. I just accepted a new office from Bill, and I couldn't do that. I couldn't go back on my word. I told him I'd take his offer." Had that call come a little earlier, I'd have been in Florida, but instead I went to Minnetonka, and that ended up strengthening the already good relationship that Bill and I had. And thanks to the unique, nontraditional compensation plan Bill had put together for me, I made a pot of money.

That deal wasn't popular with everyone, though; Bill was the vice president and general manager, but there was one guy above him in Minnesota, and he didn't like the deal. He wasn't a particularly bright man, because he didn't understand that this office had gone from losing $100K-plus to making $100,000 under my management. It was a giant turnaround, and I got a pretty good taste of it too, but they went from having a loser to a winner, and it was much more lucrative at their end then it had been. But this guy felt it was overgenerous, and as a consequence decided that he wasn't going to pay me as much.

As much as I liked the job, I wasn't interested in taking a pay cut, because that didn't seem to make sense for me. Just about this time, this guy got relocated to another part of the country, and Bill seemed to be the next logical choice in line to step up and take that guy's spot. There was a managers meeting and the corporate guys announced who the next president of Coldwell Banker was going to be—and it wasn't Bill. It was a guy that both Bill and I knew, and both Bill and I liked, but there was no way I ever could have worked for this guy. I thought I knew more about the business than he did, and Bill certainly *did* know more about the business than he did.

After that meeting, I walked down to Bill's office. I was pretty sure he'd be moving on from Coldwell after that, and I said, "I don't know where you're going, but I won't be staying. If you want to get together and kick some ideas around, let's do that." At that point, we were just colleagues, not buddies; although in an odd way we became best friends later on, we never hung out or socialized. It was odd, but it worked for us.

Bill and I had seen this brand new company RE/MAX come into the US and Canada markets, and they were making waves. As it happened, the number-one most profitable Coldwell Banker offices had been in Chicago, and RE/MAX had come into that market and kicked their ass in about two years, so we couldn't help but notice that. Bill and I talked about what we were going to do, and we agreed we'd like to get into business together. I think he gave his resignation literally two weeks after that meeting. I waited a month or so before I quit, which came right after we decided to try to purchase a RE/MAX franchise. I just couldn't work for one company while setting up another company.

Nobody actually taught me how to turn a failing company around, but I hashed out a system of my own. The first time the company sent me to turn around a failing office that was losing money, I had no idea what I was doing, and the stuff I tried at first didn't work. The second time I took an office over, I got it to be profitable by being a little bit more aggressive in how I dealt with people, and in how I recruited. By the third office, I'd had an epiphany: "I'm getting rid of people that have bad attitudes. I don't want to be around people that are negative and aren't going to make the effort. It ruins the vibe. It ruins the office." And that's when I found out that less could be more; that if you have more people but they're not interested in doing the job and you have a lesser number who are fired up about doing the job, well, that's a better deal.

I'd found my system: I'd go into the office, I'd interview every salesperson that worked there, and then after I had interviewed everyone, I'd career adjust about half of them, because they weren't selling—and, not surprisingly, the half that I kept on would sell more houses by a fair amount, thus immediately cutting our expenses and increasing productivity. Then I'd aggressively recruit to fill the empty desks.

At the last two offices I ran, I made mass career adjustments, and then went nuts recruiting. I think I fired twenty people in one day. I had the ability to recruit whole offices very quickly; I was highly aggressive and created an

> *If you have more people but they're not interested in doing the job and you have a lesser number who are fired up about doing the job, well, that's a better deal.*

environment that was appealing to other very motivated sales executives, because it was kill or be killed. Some people relished being in a more competitive environment, and those were the kinds of offices that I operated. I would never have tolerated part-timers, and if you didn't sell, you had to go. That was a different attitude for most real estate companies but it worked then, and it works today. Not everybody likes sitting in his office.

I remember once on a Saturday in November, I went into the office and saw that we only had two sales on the board for the entire month, which was awful. I was going to have to go to the manager's meeting where they'd do a roll call. When it got to me and I was asked, "How many on the board?" I was going to have to say, "Two this month," and I'd be the worst manager out of twenty. And so I called every salesperson in the office that Saturday and asked them why they weren't at work; I told them that if I hadn't sold a house, I'd be at the office on

Saturday morning. Let's just say a lot of them didn't enjoy that phone call, so they all called Bill and complained about me: "John's nuts."

I overreacted: My mistake at the time was thinking that I could change behavior. I thought, "There's a way to motivate people to sell more houses," but there really isn't. The object is to find motivated people to sell houses. Even then it's not a sure thing, but as far as your ability as a manager to change behavior or lifestyles? It's non-existent. It doesn't work. As a manager, you just don't have that kind of impact. What I learned in that office was to quit trying to change people, but instead to get rid of people who were too easily satisfied with the status quo and to hire people who wanted to get better.

At the first office, I had just hired new people, trying to start something going—and I did. It was a real office. The second office I screwed up a little bit, but eventually figured out, "I'm not going to be able to adjust the attitudes of these older people or these nonproductive people. I need to find new people with better attitudes, and then, as I find those kinds of people, I'll get rid of these people."

When you're in management or coaching, you can provide your people with everything except the most important thing; motivation.

That second office is when I came to clearly see that when you're in management or coaching, you can provide your people with everything except the most important thing; motivation.

I had motivation in spades; I woke up every day, excited about what I was doing. I was learning fast, and moving up fast; I'd found my sweet spot.

Chapter Eight

STAY FOCUSED

After all the years that I've been coaching, one thing hasn't changed: If salespeople contact more people every week, they'll sell more houses, and it's no more complicated than that. Now, there are all kinds of ways to finesse it and get better at it and create effective marketing plans—but the bottom line is that if you make more contacts, you will sell more houses.

But sales executives in real estate—or any other business—don't necessarily like making those initial contacts, and that's why they don't sell enough houses. It's the craziest conundrum, and it never changes, and that's the conundrum that I think is the whole basis of how oddly people behave, in or out of business.

There's a serious disconnect between our goals, and what we're willing to do to advance them: "I would like to quit smoking." "Okay, quit." "I can't." "Oh, okay." Or, "I would like to lose weight." "Eat less." "I can't."

It all comes back to the same thing. You know what you want—to stop drinking, to lose weight, to be more successful in work or relationships, or whatever it is you're missing or have repeatedly screwed up—but no matter how many hot coals you walk on, or diet programs you buy into, or promises you make to yourself and others, until you get yourself figured out, until you do the work to uncover what it is you don't want to face that keeps making you sabotage your own happiness—you can't stop.

> *Until you get yourself figured out, until you do the work to uncover what it is you don't want to face that keeps making you sabotage your own happiness— you can't stop.*

GETTING FOCUSED, AND STAYING THAT WAY

Understanding who you are and what you want, and staying focused on those, is a challenge a lot of people have in business or in life planning. Bill, my partner in the RE/MAX franchise, and I never lost sight of the fact we wanted to build a brokerage of significance, that we wanted to have a brokerage model that recognized the sales executive as a customer and truly would stand out in the mediocrity that sometimes can be the business.

Real estate is an "easy in" and very often a "quick out" business. It requires comparably little education to enter, as opposed to most other professions, and there are a lot of real estate brokers that will accept virtually anybody with a license, so it's relatively easy getting in. And because some people are incredibly successful in the real estate business, it looks to other people like a cinch; "Wow, I can do that." Unfortunately, it's not as easy as it looks, and many are either ill equipped from a financial standpoint to survive, or they're ill equipped to deal with the reality of what it really takes to be a successful salesperson.

The average real estate sales executive in America makes eight transactions per year—but you can't make a living on eight transactions, or provide quality representation to consumers, because it's a business that is transaction based, and doing those transactions are how you accumulate knowledge. You can read a book, you can go to class, but that isn't the same as having the actual transactional experience.

The real estate industry has always been based on high turnover; most people won't last three years, let alone five years. A lot of the business models are fine with that: "Fine. Come in, sell six, seven, eight homes. Go out of business. I made ten grand-plus on you." Actually, if they had even sold just six or seven homes, the broker would have made far more than that.

RE/MAX Results is not "easy in," and we're not "easy out." We don't hire just anybody who comes in with a license. On average, our sales executives sold twenty-three houses per person last year. When we were working out how our business would function, we decided we wanted a model that, first, would respect the sales executives who have dedicated their lives to serving their clients. By providing them with the best opportunity, the best environment, and the best tools, we also support the buyers and sellers, because if the sales executive is empowered, clearly the buyers and sellers are going to get a higher level of service and information.

We're not interested in hiring people who are short-term. We're not interested in people who aren't willing to be at this 100 percent of their time and who aren't focused. They're just not going to make it in our system and, quite frankly, wouldn't be invited into our system in the first place without those qualities. We don't hire very many new salespeople. Ninety-eight percent of our sales people are experienced, so it's a rare thing for us to hire a brand-new salesperson. They'd need to be exceptional in their experiences, their background, and their desire; they'd have to have enough economic stability to give the job a chance, and be prepared to make a time commitment until they can grow their business, both in terms of having a positive cash flow and in terms of investing money into their marketing plan.

WHY DO PEOPLE FAIL IN REAL ESTATE, OR ANY OTHER BUSINESS OR ENDEAVOR?

In my observations, the main reasons that people fail are either unrealistic expectations about what the job requires for success—"I can kind of work at this, and I'm sure I can sell some houses"—or not being able to overcome the internal roadblocks that keep them from doing what they need to do to attain the success they envision for themselves. They know what they'd like to accomplish, but don't show up willing to do what they know it takes to get there.

If you're out in your car, taking people to look at houses, you're winning. But if you're sitting at your desk playing solitaire, if you're looking at houses that you don't have buyers for, or if you're home early watching television, that's a problem. If you're not with people, if you're not willing to pick up the phone, then you're not going to succeed. Working with buyers and sellers, most people like that. *Finding* buyers and sellers, most people don't find that particularly enjoyable.

It's kind of like practice in any sport; practice isn't any fun. As Bobby Knight once observed, "Everybody wants to be on a national championship team, but nobody wants to come to practice." Everybody wants to sell a lot of houses, but nobody wants to prospect three hours a day. You have to prospect and contact your clients consistently; you can have a bad day in real estate, but you can't have a bad week, and there are specific things that you need to accomplish daily or, at a minimum, by the end of the week.

People envision how they're going to do that, but they have a hard time repeating the required behaviors day after day, even though they know logically that those behaviors will generate the financial security they want. Money will not give you happiness, but it gives you options, and it's so much easier to problem solve or to plan for your future when there are options. You're going to get financial security by working a plan and working it consistently, and "consistently" means week after week, month after month, year after year. But there's a profound disconnect with a lot of people, in terms of figuring out what they really want and accepting that they have pay a price to achieve it.

LEARN TO LISTEN

No matter what you're selling, you have to be able to listen and understand what your customer is looking for, and there are far too many salespeople who talk and don't listen. The more you listen, the more you'll understand what your client wants. The more you understand what your client wants, the better job you're going to be able to do to come up with a plan to service them.

Real estate is a service industry. The consumer can select from a wide variety of people to provide this service. You're going to have to have something that sets you apart to be selected as their service deliverer. Listening is a good way to start, but it's increasingly a lost art. We don't like to listen, we do like to pontificate, and we do like to prove to everybody that we're right and they're wrong. In sales, it's not about right or wrong. It's about understanding their needs and helping the client fulfill the needs. We work for the client. We're the one that has to understand what they're talking about when they say they want to downsize, what they're talking about when they say that they need more room. What are they really saying?

Listening better can help you to discern what clients really want, as opposed to what they may think they want. For instance, so often clients will have geographic restraints on where they want to buy, but those ideas are often based upon misinformation, or lack of understanding about what other, possibly better, opportunities are. Their criteria may be legitimate, but we also need to ask more questions—"Help me understand. Why would you feel that would be the only place that you would be able to find a house that you would want to live in?"— and we've got to find out what they're after. Sometimes the answer is, "Well, because I heard that's got the best school district." That may not be correct, and if it's not and you know it and can explain where the better school districts are located, then you've done them a service and opened up a lot more possibilities.

> *Listening better can help you to discern what clients really want, as opposed to what they may think they want.*

When I'm buying houses for myself, I'm looking to work with somebody who sells a lot of real estate. I'm looking for somebody who is a careful listener, who hears what I'm saying and is willing to take direction. And I'm looking for somebody that has integrity and honesty, along with the skills required to follow up and get the sale done expeditiously.

I'm looking for somebody who knows I'm the client. I'm looking for somebody who has a good base of knowledge, knows the market, knows the players, knows current trends, and who knows what's good and what's not good in the marketplace, whom I can trust to honestly point out the positives and negatives about houses that I'm attracted to.

I need to like the person. They don't need to be my buddy, but I have to like them. I don't like doing business with people I don't like. They have to be reasonable, presentable, and positive.

FOCUS ON WHAT YOU KNOW

When somebody pitches to me, "John, I've got a friend who's doing a medical start up; this thing could go through the moon, and if you invest, you've got a shot at hitting the jackpot," my answer to that is, "Thanks, but no thanks," because I don't know anything about the medical field, so it's not where I'd spend my money.

But if somebody calls me up and says, "Boy, I ran across this little building that is so undervalued because they just haven't figured out how to get the right tenant in it," I might go look at that building. I might not buy it, but I'd look at that building, because that's something I understand. I'm not afraid of being speculative, I'm not afraid of taking chances, but I don't go outside of my knowledge area. I don't give my money to other people to invest. I don't like it. It's not who I am. Is that right or wrong? I have an old friend who put every dime he could make into Apple stock. He's a financial star now.

I didn't know what Apple stock was when he was buying it; I didn't even know how to work a computer at the time. Does that make him smarter than I am? Well, it makes him a better investor than I am, but that's not me. That's not what I'm good at or focused on.

It's a question of understanding who you are and what makes you feel good. For me, giving my money to stockbrokers and then having them call me to tell me my portfolio was way down wasn't making me feel good. I've never yet been cheated or lost money on a piece of real estate. Are some deals better than others? Yep. Are there some that are more of a headache than others? Yep. But I know real estate, so I know that if I buy it, run it, keep it, and pay for it, I won.

That's why a real estate career isn't for everybody. That's why going to work as a personal trainer isn't for everybody. That's why being a writer isn't for everybody. Because we all have different innate desires, and we have to figure out if we can get our behavior to match up with our desires. If your behavior doesn't match your desires, then you either have to change your behavior or change your desires, because there are only two things in the equation.

> *If your behavior doesn't match your desires, then you either have to change your behavior or change your desires, because there are only two things in the equation.*

If you want to do one particular thing and it's not working, you have to find out why you can't make that work, and either alter your behavior, or find something else to do. Not everyone is cut out to do sales work, for instance; I have people in management in my company who would never want to sell houses, but boy, they sure can administer a title insurance company because of their attention to numbers and detail, and they're highly valued for those abilities.

BECOME AN OPTIMIST

Every business has its challenges. In real estate, the recent recession was deeper than anyone had expected it to be, but I stuck it out by being optimistic. For me, optimism was learned behavior; I never had a role model for optimism, but as a student of history I knew a rise was inevitable. We're not sentenced to the attitudes toward life that we grew up with; we can learn better ones.

What keeps us from being optimistic? One of the most difficult things for people to overcome on a day-to-day basis is the bombardment of information we get from the so-called media. It's ignorant, misinformed, and destructive so much of the time. It's so easy to be panicked, and to see the world around us as a more negative, more dangerous place than it is. But empirically speaking, the world is a better place than it's ever been. There's more opportunity for more people than there's ever been. It's safer than it's ever been. We're living longer than people ever dreamed they would. We're closing in on Utopia, but if you listen to the news tonight, you aren't going to think it's a Utopia. You're going to think the world's coming to an end.

In the throes of the last recession, people were saying, "We're never going to come back from this. It's a new era," but that's just baloney. Read your history books: There are always ups and downs, there's always change, but human beings remain human beings. Some of them are good. Some of them are skunks. Some of them are leaders. Some of them are followers. But what humans are overall doesn't change much.

When we're in a downward market, the first thing we have to do is stabilize our business so we don't go out of business, and next we have to figure out how we can prosper with this negativity, because there are always opportunities to prosper. One answer in an upmarket like this one is to bankroll cash so that you're positioned to buy the next time there's a recession and you're presented with opportunities. But the real trick is to never lose sight of the fact that no matter what you read or hear other people saying, opportunities do exist.

DON'T GET HOOKED ON PLAYING THE VICTIM

Some people don't look for those opportunities or practice optimism, and instead put their energy into seeing themselves as victims, using that victimhood as a "Get Out of Jail Free" card for all their poor choices: "The reason I rob people is because I'm poor," or, "The reason I'm a drug addict is because I didn't have two parents," etc., etc. Are these issues factors in how screwed up your life is? Maybe—but the fact is that everybody that's poor doesn't steal, and everybody that had a broken family doesn't end up becoming a heroin addict. Those are all choices. We like to blame society for the choices that individuals make, when the reality is that they have an opportunity to take care of themselves. Self-reliance used to be a highly prized virtue, but it's been replaced to a large extent by self-absolution.

I was listening on the radio the other day to an old Merle Haggard song. I'm not a big country western guy, but I had that station on, and Merle was talking about how he's proud to be a working man; as long as his hands worked, he was going to make a living, and you'd never see him on welfare; that, by gosh, he was going to take care of himself, his wife, and his kids, and he was proud of that. We've lost a lot of that attitude, and it's a shame. Your first aspiration should be to take care of yourself and your family, and anything after that is a bonus. But we somehow skip the hard part and go right to, "Why aren't there more bonuses?" And everybody doesn't get a bonus. There are no guarantees. You have to come up with something extra, something different. Everybody doesn't get to have the great life. You get to have a life, an opportunity, and that's what you get. The rest is up to you.

People start out with unrealistic expectations around life. I often see that in younger people who don't know how hard it was for their family members or role models to achieve what they did. Because of their ability to navigate a college education, they assume that will translate into easing the next steps in life, and often there's no correlation between those two things. While a college education certainly provides you with information and opportunity to grow and experience new things and is an advantage, it is far from providing all the answers most of us need in our careers.

REBOOT YOUR WORK ETHIC

I've told some pretty negative stories on my dad in this book, but like all people, there was more than one side to him. The non-chemically dependent side was significant in its knowledge of different things. My dad made it very clear to me that he wouldn't give me anything. He did suggest he would help pay for school if I wanted to go to college, because he did for my sister, but I wasn't college oriented. He made it very clear that whatever I wanted in life I'd have to go work for, and that he had neither the ability nor the desire to provide stuff for me. He wasn't going to buy me a car. He wasn't going to buy me a house. He wasn't going to take me on vacations. What I wanted, I'd have to find a way to provide for myself.

This implanted a work ethic that has stood me in good stead. There have been a number of times in my life when I held down two jobs. It didn't seem odd; when I started in real estate, I thought, "I want to be a real estate sales executive, and yet I've got to pay for my house, so I guess I've got to do two things, and I guess I've got to work sixteen hours a day." And did I feel sorry for myself? No; actually, I kind of dug it. I was learning something new. I was transitioning from one spot to the other.

People are often unrealistic about the sacrifices you need to make if you're clear on what you want. And I was pretty clear, once I sobered up, that I wanted financial security. I didn't even know what it meant when I was in my late or mid-twenties. I just knew that it was better to have money than not to have money. I didn't get where it was going to come from or how I was going to do it, but it was clear to me that there was a benefit to financial security. I hadn't understood the idea of money providing me with options, or how having it meant I could impact others' lives for the better. I wasn't even near there in personal development. But I knew I'd be better off with it than I would be without it.

FOCUS ON YOUR *WHY*

Your focus has to be on why you're doing what you're doing. Is the potential reward worth the effort? If it is, then you have to be committed to doing whatever it is you must do to achieve progress every day; that, once again, you can have a bad day, but you can't have a bad week, and you certainly can't have a bad month. So if you screw up one day because of health, because of an emergency, or because of other distractions, then you have to brush yourself off and get back on schedule the next day. You can't let it spiral into tentativeness about your strategy to achieve your goals, and that's hard for people to do.

It's easy to get distracted. Our world is full of distractions, more by the day, but they have nothing to do with the big picture. You have to be able to unplug yourself from all the drivel that the media and other people push at you, because it is ultimately destructive and the distraction will derail your efforts to move forward.

The joy of working on what you want to do is every bit as satisfying as the achievement. If you don't get the same joy out of doing it as you will on achieving it, then you're in the wrong place in your life, because the achievement may not ever occur, so the joy has to be in the doing.

As I write this, I'm at the opposite end of the state from where I was earlier in the week. I have an incredibly long drive on the way back home again today from my business. I couldn't be happier. I'm just happy. Why? Because I'm doing what I want to do. It's been a challenging day, but that's life. I didn't have any groundbreaking triumphs today. No mountains were climbed. It was just a day in the life, and I loved it.

> *If you don't get the same joy out of doing it as you will on achieving it, then you're in the wrong place in your life, because the achievement may not ever occur, so the joy has to be in the doing.*

You have to come up with a way to love the days in your life, and love the work you do for its own sake. Figure that out, and the rest of it will follow.

THE POWER OF NO

When we talk about having success in business as well as a balance in personal life, you have to be willing to use the power of the word NO in order to meet your own personal needs. What I mean by that is when we talk about how you design your business plan, how you design your life plan, the first and foremost thing is that you have to take care of yourself, because you can't take care of your personal and business responsibilities or of the people who matter in your life if you're not in a good place both mentally and physically.

In the real estate business, sales executives sometimes become obsessed with the idea of customer service. I agree that the most important thing is the customer; our sales executives are the most important people to the brokerage and the customer is the most important person to the sales executive. However, that doesn't mean that you drop everything immediately to respond to whatever somebody thinks is a need, or that if you have scheduled time to take your kids to Pizza World on Wednesday night, you can't tell a customer "I'm sorry. I'm not available Wednesday night. Would Friday or Saturday work better for you?"

Sometimes it's even appropriate for you to decline an appointment with a client. As a real estate sales executive, I never ran out to show a house. If somebody wanted to see a house I had listed, they were going to meet me at the office first. If they didn't want to invest that time to meet me at the office and do a little preliminary qualification to make sure that they were appropriate for this particular house, then I didn't show them the house.

Some people consider that almost blasphemous, but my answer to that is **no**.

I look at my time management in the same way. I work fifty-five hours a week. I've divided up my job into three different categories, and I allot a percentage of those hours to each of them. My support person and I fill those spots, and when they're full, whatever else comes up is pushed back to the next week and sometimes to the week after that. I don't jump to disrupt my schedule to do what somebody thinks is an urgent activity. I do have the right and sometimes even the responsibility to say, "No. I'm sorry I'm unavailable, but I can do it X or Y."

When we talk about **no**, we're talking about having some control over your time management and your personal life; not to the extent that you don't fulfill your expectations for how many hours or how much work you're going to put in, in a workweek, but that you do have the right to say "No. I can't do that. No. I'm not available for that. No. I'm not interested in that." Volunteerism is a good example; I'm very active in the community, and there's one organization that I adore and support with all the energy I have. But when they asked me to be on their board of directors, my answer was "Thank you so much, but no." It's not that I don't support them; it's simply that I can't take on one more thing.

That's not in the cards for me because of the way I do my time management, the way I do my job, and the time I set aside for my family. The time for that commitment is just not there; it might be five years from now, but I don't feel guilty saying **no** now because it doesn't fit into the big plan. Becoming confident in your plan and what you're trying to accomplish, you do have to be ready, willing, and able to say, "No. I'm sorry, I can't do that."

THINK ABOUT IT:

What's standing between you and your goals? Usually, it's focus: focus on not just the goals, but

also on the many small steps it takes to get from here to there.

- **Are you clear about your goals?** Or are they general and too nebulous to focus on? There's a difference between saying something general like, "I want to look better," versus, "I want to lose twenty pounds by Christmas." There's a difference between saying, "I want to be more literate," and deciding, "I'm going to read one classic book a month." In both cases, the second goal is more likely to be achievable, because it's clearly stated and suggests a series of steps that can accomplish it.

- **Are you clear on what stops you from keeping the promises you make to yourself?** I've talked at length about the importance of therapy throughout this book, at least in how it impacted and improved my life. If you can't think of another reason to go, the best one might be finding out why you can't stay focused long enough to achieve your goals.

- **Don't play the victim card—not because you're not a victim, but because it shouldn't define who you are.** Everyone has pain; everyone has a story about how they got to be who they are, and that's fine. But don't let the past dictate your future, especially if the past has been unpleasant. People may feel sorry for you, or say they do, but the fact is, playing the victim card won't advance you an inch toward your goals.

- **Turn away from distractions, because they eat time.** Put yourself on a social media/ television/

talk show diet. Use the time doing something that will advance you, not distract you.

- **Learn to say no, and stick with it.** Part of being focused is managing your time well. If you can't say no when people are intruding on your schedule, then you'll wind up living on theirs.

Chapter Nine

A BETTER MAN

Before his death in 1994, a remarkable thing happened between my father and me; we were able to mend fences. He'd cut back his drinking to nearly nothing, because his body just couldn't take it anymore. My mom didn't drink like she had in the past, either. It made things nominally more peaceable, and he and I were able to spend time together, talking. I'd changed, he'd changed, and time and experience had given us both some needed perspective. We were finally able to reach across the divide created by years of anger and disappointment, and see each other as we were: two imperfect people looking to make peace with our lives.

I hadn't really understood until he finally retired how much my dad had hated his job. Now I saw that the longer my dad didn't work at the chemical factory, the happier he got. You know how you hear about how retirement isn't good for people? He wasn't that person; he thrived in retirement. He loved doing nothing. He loved going to the bakery, or sitting in his chair, listening to opera. He loved planting stuff in the backyard. He and my mom still bickered, although it no longer got physical. Sometimes, I'd yell at my dad for being a jerk to my mom. But then two weeks later, I'd have to yell at my mom for being a jerk to my dad, because she could just nag the hell out of him. It was their private dance, the moves learned through long years of marriage.

My dad kept track of everything that happened in my business. Every newspaper article he could find that featured my offices or me—anything that mentioned my name—my dad knew about it, and the level of pride he had in my accomplishments in running this business was off the charts. He was in the hospital after a rough surgery when I bought my first big office building, and I went to see him after visiting hours to tell him about it. He was on a respirator, and he'd had his vocal cords removed years earlier because of esophageal cancer, so he couldn't talk. But when I went to see him again the following day, he painstakingly laid out all of these little pieces of paper for me, and I saw that he'd done an amortization schedule of the mortgage. He had analyzed the property in terms of how to handle it on a tax basis and how to deduct the basis points, all on these little scraps of paper. He didn't have a calculator. He was just that good at math. He truly admired how I'd overcome my issues, and had a lot of respect for me.

Yet here's an odd thing; my dad left Earth without ever telling his wife or his kids or his grandkids that he loved them. He just couldn't say those words, and not just after losing his vocal chords—but when you saw him with his two grandsons, he was clearly on another planet of happiness. I remember a birthday he had, close to the time when he died; we had his birthday party in the hospital, and as those two rug rats were jumping all over his bed, Dad's face was one big smile.

He didn't last long after that. I'd sit with him and hold his hand when he was really struggling, and I'd tell him I loved him. He'd squeeze my hand so hard I thought my fingers would pop. But he never could say the words.

When Dad died, my mom told us she didn't want to live anymore: "Life isn't going to be any good without your dad." My sister and I got her a cat—she'd always wanted one after our last cat had died, but Dad had wanted the freedom to travel, and preferred not having the responsibility to care for another pet. They became best friends, Mom and this old rescue cat. After a few months, my mom was the happiest she'd ever been in her life, living by herself in her house with the cat.

Bill and I continued to build our business, and it was a good one. We worked together seamlessly, and lived in the same upmarket neighborhood, although we almost never saw each other outside of working hours. Our friendship was work based, and though we liked and admired each other, our social lives were separate. That's why it was odd when, one weekend afternoon, he called me at home to say, "I have to come over and talk to you." That meant it was serious. I assumed it had to do with his health: Bill had fought a long, rough battle with cancer that had started in his colon and spread to his liver. He had tried as hard as a man could, given those cards. He never wanted to throw in the towel, though the chemo and radiation had made it tough for him. His effectiveness was greatly diminished in his last few years, but his effort and desire were not diminished.

Bill got to my house in a few minutes, and the two of us sat down. Without much preamble, he laid it out for me: although treatment had allowed him many years of life, there was now no more that his doctors could do for him. The clock was ticking; he hadn't much longer to live.

That's when he asked me for what he called "the biggest favor anybody could ask": He wanted me to tear up our buy/sell agreement, to allow him to leave his half of company to his son, and to change the beneficiary of our life insurance to his son, so that the money we intended to go to fund the buy-sell would go to his wife. That meant his wife would get the value of the company, and his son would get half the company. The legacy piece was important to him; Bill wanted to know that his son would carry on the Saunders name in Collopy-Saunders Real Estate.

Granting him this favor would cost me millions. I'd never dreamed of having that much money in my life, let alone that somebody would come in my living room and ask me to give it to his son and his wife.

But I barely hesitated before saying, "Okay."

To understand why I agreed, you have to go back to the way I grew up, with my sensibility of blue-collar right and wrong, and the tremendous amount of loyalty that we felt toward our friends and the guys in the neighborhood. As odd as our relationship was sometimes, Bill and I were best friends. Now my best friend was asking for something that clearly meant a lot to him—and he was dying. In that moment, I didn't stop to evaluate whether asking for this was right or wrong, fair or unfair. I just was sitting in a room with a guy I cared about. We had certainly had our ups and downs in our relationship, but I knew that I wouldn't have been there, if he had not been with me in the beginning. It was just that simple. We're the largest RE/MAX in the world right now, but none of it could have happened without Bill. He had been the most important person in my business life, and I owed him.

That said, I had some second (and third) thoughts about my answer after he'd left and in the following days. In fact, the more I thought about it, the more I felt he never should have made such an enormous request. I talked to my accountant, told him the story, and he said, "You're nuts." I talked to another friend, someone from my X-rated days who's now a high-powered criminal attorney and one of the few people I would trust with my life. There have been many times when I've gone to him with emotional, personal, or financial questions to just get his opinion, because there's not that many people whose advice I'm prepared to take. His response was similar to the accountant's, but delivered in much more colorful language.

Now, in my heart, I was blaming Bill for asking me. I was falling into the "victim" mindset—and not necessarily taking responsibility for not having the balls to say "No" or at least asking for more time to think on it. I was vacillating, thinking, "Well, he's not going to die tomorrow. What would our relationship have been like if I'd have said no?" I knew that he had an advantage; there always was a part of me that wanted his approval, that wanted him to say, "Man, that John's really something. I'm the luckiest guy in the world to have him for a partner," though he'd never have said that, because that's not who he was. Still, I didn't want to disappoint him, and I didn't want a confrontation with him.

As I began to second-guess the decision, anger began building in my head. What a jerk Bill was for asking this of me! The more I thought about it, the madder I got. At this point in my life I hadn't addressed my anger management issues, and now this festering, toxic rage was seeping into other areas of my life, because I was just pissed about everything. I was pissed about work. I was pissed that this came up. I was pissed that Bill was dying. I felt like a dummy for having gone down that road: *What are you, a chicken? You couldn't say "no"? Are you stupid?*

Fortunately, I was in therapy, so I thoroughly talked this through with my therapist, because this was really bugging me. And eventually I came to grips with the fact that I had two choices: I could renege and tell Bill I'd changed my mind, because we hadn't signed the paperwork yet. Or, I could go forward and honor what I had said I would do.

So after hashing it all out with a few more people, and after many hours of reflection on it on my own, I decided to honor the commitment I'd made. It took more work and time, but with the help of my therapist, I forgave Bill for asking, and I accepted responsibility for what I had done in agreeing to his request. I decided I would turn this into a net positive by embracing his son, whom I knew slightly as one of our salespeople. Maybe this new young partner would help the company grow, and selling him my half of the business might provide my own exit plan down the line. I committed to doing everything in my power to make this work.

And so we start on a new era. With Bill's passing, his son and I starting to work together as partners. I tried to be optimistic; I delegated a tremendous amount of decision making to him. He selected a couple of sites where he thought we should open new offices, and I treated him very much like an equal.

But our business styles simply didn't mesh, neither did our personalities, and his methods sometimes struck me as unorthodox. Bill and I had had our ways of doing things, and rules about decision making. We saw the business in a similar way, and that made it easy to agree. Certainly, his son's ideas were sometimes innovative—but they weren't always in line with what I thought was the right way to do things, and the control I'd had over the business was eroding fast.

The company was growing as the economy began to turn around, and we were making some major acquisitions. But in terms of my job satisfaction and what I felt about having a business partner, things were not so great. Clearly, he wasn't comfortable with my style, either: He found me overly blunt, emotional, and abrasive, a bad match with his more-detached, dispassionate personality. I'm easier going now than I was then; a combination of therapy, age, and happiness has made me less explosive and angry than I used to be. But at that point I was still pretty hotheaded—unhappy over the loss of my friend/business partner, unhappy over issues of the company directions and control. This mutually unfortunate partnership was making it worse, because I didn't really have anyone to blame but myself for getting into it. And, in retrospect, the business wasn't a good fit for him; his father's dream wasn't his. We'd both been left with a legacy that neither of us really wanted. Where I loved and still love real estate, he saw it as a less-creative, less-interesting career than he'd hoped to have.

We struggled on for a number of years; we hashed out an agreement that, given my more extensive experience, I'd continue to be the one mostly running things until I turned sixty-six, at which point we agreed he could buy me out and I'd cut back on my hours and semi-retire. It seemed like a workable plan, and it provided me with the exit strategy I wanted.

But problems kept cropping up; the trust between us continued to erode, and it didn't help that he wasn't consulting with his partners as he had been asked to do (and had agreed to do) ahead of making important business decisions that impacted us all. Our relationship had gone from bad to worse, and it plainly wasn't sustainable. It was a poorly arranged marriage that just wasn't working out.

The two of us had regularly scheduled Tuesday meetings where we would get together and talk about the week's work. At one of those Tuesday meetings, he walked in the room, he wrote a number on the board and said, "I'm done. That's what it takes to buy me out." And he left.

Thus, within a four-year period, I had to buy the company *again*, and he got paid twice. I have no idea if his dad and he had a scheme, as some people subsequently suggested, but I doubt it; I think his dad was sincere in wanting the business to be his legacy, and that his son just didn't care enough to carry on his father's desires and legacy. Now the son was up another $3 million, but I was the sole owner.

I realize this is one of the most ridiculous business stories I've ever heard, much less had to tell on myself. Who would do such a crazy thing? That said, if I had to make that choice again today, I believe I'd still have said yes to Bill, because it was the right thing to do. Nothing happened that I'm embarrassed about; I honored my word and did the best I could do. But the good news is that once I'd orchestrated the finances to buy him out, my life just got better and better and better—and that hasn't stopped. The company culture immediately got much less tense and stressful; I was frankly much happier without a partner than I had been with the wrong partner, and I'm sure he felt the same way about not working with me.

Even the worst situations can have some upside if you look for it, and this one was no exception: One great thing that's come out of all of this is that we've started a major charity, the Results Foundation. We're raising hundreds of thousands of dollars to go back into the communities where our offices are located, and that's not something I could have explained to him as a partner. When I retire, half of my assets (including the company) are going into a trust that will continue to fund this foundation. Currently, a portion of every one of our real estate transactions from mortgage and title goes toward the Results Foundation. Our sales executives contribute, too.

The first thing we did in setting up the charity's work was to establish the Bill Saunders Memorial Scholarship Fund. I know how important it was to my old friend Bill that he be remembered in some meaningful way, and while the scholarship fund might not have been the legacy that he had originally envisioned, I think he would have been pleased to see his name attached to such a good cause. Additionally, our executive committee has selected a number of community-based charities,

> *Currently, a portion of every one of our real estate transactions from mortgage and title goes toward the Results Foundation.*

like the Cancer Society's local Walk for Life fundraisers that we're also supporting. We're not looking to reinvent the wheel; we're partnering with others who have already established worthy causes that give back to the community. When I pass on, the foundation is likely going to have a value of around $10 to $15 million, plus a cash flow of up to $3 million a year.

We're going to keep increasing the size of our company and our ancillary services so that number keeps getting bigger and bigger, and more flows back through the foundation to the community. When I leave RE/MAX Results, I'll still be the chairman of the board, but I'll be spending more time at the Results Foundation, raising funds. In fact, any profits from the sale of this book and any subsequent speaking I do about it will also be going straight to the foundation.

My friends ask me why I don't just stop doing what I do, and enjoy life. But I don't fish.

I like golf, but not that much. I like what I do; I like helping people build a career. I like helping people and empowering them so they can represent buyers and sellers. Added to that is that we are truly building something that is going to give back and change lives.

I've never though of myself as any kind of a philanthropist. I've never considered myself to be altruistic. I'm pretty pragmatic; some people would even say I'm kind of a hard ass. And I know I'm not going to live forever, but the thought that I'm contributing to something worthwhile and positive that will outlive me is enormously satisfying. I don't know when my values switched around to embrace that as a goal, but I do know that that gives me the desire to go to work every day. I realize it sounds dorky, but this is truly my definition of a win-win: We make money, our sales executives make money, our staff has a great place to work, and we help people? That sounds like a pretty good deal for everybody. I don't see any downside to it.

Chapter Ten

WHAT YOU SAY AND WHAT YOU DO

I n my observations, there are three things all people want. They want to be happy and have serenity in their lives. They want to have financial security. And they want their kids to have it better than they did.

But what they say only rarely lines up with what they do—and that's a problem. Too often, they're looking for someone or something else, some outside agency, to step up and wave a wand and fix it or fix them. All of us have ideas and expectations around what it would take to bring us real happiness, and a lot of those are unrealistic. "Happily ever after" only happens in storybooks, but we're always looking for it, and most people believe that their personal happiness hangs on some circumstance that's beyond their control; some "If only…" connected to love or opportunity or other externals.

That isn't what makes you happy. It's a contributor to your life and can impact you, but the only control you have over happiness is *you*. You will determine whether you're happy or not.

There's a book that I give out to participants in a class I teach, written by a national radio host, Dennis Prager, called *Happiness Is a Serious Problem*. It focuses in on the fact that it's your job to be happy, but that it takes an effort, and it takes awareness. It takes determination to be happy. It doesn't simply appear. It doesn't come from magic. It doesn't come from external things, like getting a raise or your kid making the basketball team or your spouse being a knockout. None of those are really what happiness is about. Most people are searching for some sort of peace and joy in life, yet if you ask them to define it, much less what they're doing to contribute to it, they're stumped.

As a person who coaches people in business, I can tell you that while most people can visualize what they want to accomplish in business, when they're given the steps they need to take in order to achieve it, the vast majority of them just won't follow the steps. Look at the numbers of people who smoke, drink, do drugs, get divorced, have extramarital affairs, or cheat on their taxes; none of those things are going to promote their happiness. Yet they give in to their desires for immediate gratification, rather than thinking through the long-term consequences of what they're choosing to do.

DON'T UNDERESTIMATE THE POWER OF FORGIVING OTHERS

I met with someone earlier one day, one of my sales executives, whose family situation is so far beyond turmoil there's not a word for it: deaths, heartbreak upon heartbreak, and terrible losses, none of which she'd brought on herself. But when I met with her, she had accepted what had happened to her and was figuring out how to deal with it. And so, as traumatized as she is that her life has been shaken to the very core, she has already hit bottom, she is already moving forward, she is now living life a day at a time, she has reached out in a couple different areas for support, and is trying to understand what happened so she can deal with it. She had come to me not for sympathy, not to place blame, but for financial advice.

What happened to her will never leave her heart. She will always have this horrific, traumatic experience in her past, but she is going to get through this—and she's going to come out of the other side stronger, smarter, and happier. Now, "happier" doesn't mean that she won't remember the bad things that happened to her. We don't forget about people who have wronged us. We don't forget about experiences that were catastrophic. We don't forget about them, but we accept them, even if we can't fully understand them. If some of them happened to us because of the actions of another person, our only choice is to forgive them if we are to move forward. I don't hate what happened to me when I was younger, not the difficulties I've had or the times I've been broke or the times I was embarrassed. I learned from those situations, and I've moved on. There's not one person on the face of the Earth that doesn't have difficult life events. The question is, how are they going to apply to the next twenty-four hours in your life, a day at a time?

> *There's not one person on the face of the Earth that doesn't have difficult life events. The question is, how are they going to apply to the next twenty-four hours in your life, a day at a time?*

CHOOSE HAPPINESS

How do we move forward? By choosing to make happiness in the world around us—and that is a choice, and a powerful one. As an example, we had a gathering for one of our experienced sales executives; Mike has been with me for almost thirty years, and he had just sold his hundreth condo in the same development, so we had a nice little party for him here at the office. We all took forty-five minutes out of our life to go, "Damn. Never heard of anybody who sold that many condos in one place," and that's just how simple life is. Everyone in the room paid their respects to him and got a smile on their face, and then we were back to work. And that's how you lead your life a day at a time. Not, "Geez. I wonder if he's too old. Gee. I wonder if he'll ever sell a condo again?" None of that had to do with that day. That day was, "We're going to celebrate him for his accomplishment."

It wasn't until afterward that I found out that one of our younger sales executives gave him the listing because she knew it was his dream to get to one hundred. She handed it to him because she wanted to see him win—and she didn't tell anyone about it. Now, he'd probably have hit that number on his own in six months or a year, because he's still active, but here another person who reached out and made it happen for him; we all got a kick out of it, and Mike was floating around the office on a cloud of happiness. Imagine the good feelings bubbling over in that generous younger person's heart, for having orchestrated that moment for him. That's the kind of behavior that makes all of us happier. Everything in that exchange produced happiness—so why don't we do more things that produce happiness if we want to be happy?

ARE YOU HELPING YOURSELF IN BIG WAYS, OR SABOTAGING YOURSELF IN SMALL WAYS?

Just as small acts of kindness can create joy for others and ourselves, small careless acts can sabotage us if we're unaware of their consequences. People often don't see that the little things they do can undermine their larger goals. If you ask someone, they'll tell you that they'd like to be able to take care of themselves and their family. But I've found through my own unscientific survey that when I ask a person, "How much money do you spend at Starbucks?" versus, "How much money did you put in the bank this month?" a surprising number of people spend more money at Starbucks than they put in the bank. Clearly, that doesn't contribute to doing what they say they want to do. We match our employees' 401(k) investments, but only about 18 percent of them take advantage of that. What's more important, seeing two hundred and fifty channels of cable TV and Netflix, or funding your IRA for when you're sixty-five years old? The same people who'll tell you they want financial security will also tell you, "I can't live without cable TV." But they could—and, arguably, they could live better.

NOTHING TRUMPS PERSONAL RESPONSIBILITY

Recently, I was listening to somebody being interviewed who was talking about how he felt that he was owed health care, and that it's the government's responsibility to provide it for him. Growing up, I never thought the government owed me anything. What are the chances that this guy being interviewed is willing to work two jobs to get ahead? I'd guess zero. Ronald Reagan said, "We want to reject the idea that every time a law is broken, society is guilty, rather than the lawbreaker. It's time to restore the American precept that each individual is accountable for his actions."

I talked earlier about our country's new millionaires, many of whom came from countries where the deck was stacked against them and where that kind of upward mobility wasn't even a possibility. They get here, and they're willing and eager to work hard, because they're grateful for the opportunity to achieve their dreams and provide a brighter future for their families. Yet we have people here who are second- and third- and fourth-generation Americans, who are saying, "I just want healthcare. Give me more healthcare," not, "What's the best opportunity? How can I prosper? How do I work harder, smarter, more? What can I do that will help me to succeed?"

Most people if asked will tell you they want their children to prosper, and to be better off than they were—yet the way my generation raised their children and the way the next generation appears to be raising their children is not designed to inspire or empower them or support their efforts to rise. Look at the number of Millennials still living at home. In the past, the idea of growing up included getting a job, moving out, and finding your place in the world—but somehow we've made it socially acceptable to live off of your parents as an adult. Can you imagine in our grandparents' day, if twenty-somethings were saying, "Mom, Dad, can you pay for me to go to college?" With the exception of the upper classes, I guarantee you the majority of young people didn't expect, much less demand, that kind of support from their folks. My dad got to college by fighting in World War II, and going to school on the G.I. Bill—and you can still get that deal. If you don't have enough money to go to college and you want to go, go into the military for four years. I've got a hunch you're going to be a better college student when you come out than you would have been if you had gone at age eighteen with Mom and Dad paying for it.

We say we want our kids to prosper, but we're not willing to tell them, "I think it's time for you to pick a direction in life, and I'm here to support your direction, but I'm not here to finance your direction, or to keep you from being self-sufficient." We're doing them a disservice. We're denying them the opportunity to develop the kind of work ethic that will guarantee their survival.

ARE YOU WORKING TOWARD YOUR GOALS, OR JUST MAKING EXCUSES?

We're all free to daydream and say, "This is what I'd like. This is what I wish we could have. This is how I wish things would go," but then when we look at the ten or eleven or twelve hours that we were awake the day before, what percentage of those hours will ultimately contribute to the fulfillment of our goals of being happy, of having financial security, or of making sure our kids do better than we did?

Instead, we fall into habits that aren't good for us and will subtract from our lives, not bring us closer to what we want; bad habits around time management, around diet and exercise, and around substance abuse. Most people who drink a lot won't come out and say that they want to die earlier, but they will—and meanwhile they're wasting money that could have been spent productively somewhere. They're undermining themselves,

> *Most people who drink a lot won't come out and say that they want to die earlier, but they will—and meanwhile they're wasting money that could have been spent productively somewhere.*

and creating failure, without being willing to take responsibility for it when it comes.

I have had numerous failures: I've had business failures. I've had relationship failures. I've had legal failures. I've had moral failures. But do you know whose fault every one of those failures was? Mine. It wasn't the economy. It wasn't this bad person I married. It wasn't because I was cheated, or because of any other bad break I had along the way.

It was me.

If I was cheated, it's because I let myself be cheated. So the cheater may be a skunk, but the fault is with me because I wasn't paying attention. And I may have had troubles with Wife #1, but I sure was a jerk to Wife #1. The way those things ended up was because of me.

Those kinds of things take a while for people to own up to. One of the positive things that you learn in legitimate treatment programs is to stop blaming other people and look to yourself, not only for how you got to where you are, but how you're going to move forward.

There are so many opportunities for us to learn from our life experiences, to learn from the people around us, and to apply what we learn to creating behaviors that will help us reach the goals we have. Yes, it's difficult to turn behavior around; after you've been somebody for fifteen, twenty, or thirty years, you aren't going to change it all in three months. It may take you ten years, but you can get better. AA taught me some things that have been the cornerstones of my own recovery; but the wisdom of the Serenity Prayer and the notion of living one day at a time are ideas that apply to everyone, not just to people in recovery.

The only thing you can count on in life is that it will be challenging. All of us are going to have friends and family who die. All of us are going to have trauma related to life experiences. Our job gets eliminated. The economy flounders. We're going to have health problems. All these things are going to happen to each and every one of us, and more than once.

You shouldn't be surprised when bad stuff happens, and you shouldn't be overwhelmed when it happens. You should be getting busy, getting your options in line. Once again, "Money will not give you happiness, but money does give you options." Granted that we're going to have problems in our lives, but when you have financial security, you'll have more ways to deal with the problems, and more choices about how to solve them. You can get a second opinion at the Mayo Clinic. You can hire a better lawyer. You can get a tutor for your child. You can move to a safer neighborhood. Money gives you options.

YOU CAN'T CARE FOR OTHERS IF YOU CAN'T TAKE CARE OF YOURSELF

I'm looking for ways that I can leverage what I've accomplished into A) helping myself, B) helping my family, C) helping the people I work with, and D) giving back to the community. That's the order, and I'm not ashamed to put myself at the top of the list—because if I don't take care of myself, I can't help any of those other people.

If you don't take care of yourself—if you don't manage your relationship with your significant other, if you're not there for your kids, if you don't have a moral system of beliefs— you're not going to be able to go to work and be your best. It is not selfish to put your self-care first—it's essential. You have to find time for yourself, or you will not be able to stand up to the day-to-day stuff that happens.

If you're a mess and something bad happens, then you're more likely to react poorly to that event. If you're on solid emotional footing, you will face it, you will deal with it, and ultimately you'll learn from it. It doesn't mean it won't be hard. It doesn't mean you won't hurt. It doesn't mean you won't shed a tear. But you will deal with it, and you'll deal with it more effectively, and in the future that experience will forge your character.

How many times have we heard a story about athletes who had every tool necessary to become stars, but didn't, either because of personal life or work habits? They could've been among the greatest, but their head wasn't screwed on straight. And then there are other guys who weren't quite as talented, but who outworked their more-gifted peers at building their skills, and ended up making the major leagues. I see that every day; the gaps between people in terms of their appearance and skills isn't that wide—but between their degrees of desire and determination, there are huge differences.

I don't know why that is; as I've said before, you cannot motivate people. If you have a sales executive who just isn't into it, then you are not going to be able to help them get into it. What you need to do for that person is help them go find a new job, because if there's not that spark of desire and the vision, they've got no shot. They may bullshit themselves about it, but that's the fact.

Remember the sales executive I talked about at the opening of this chapter, whose life had taken a hard turn for the worse? She's still very much on my mind as I write this, and I know I'll never be the same person I was before I talked with her. I'm changed. Listening to her had a permanent impact on my psyche. Hearing about what happened to her and witnessing her intestinal fortitude about wanting to get control of her life again is one of those experiences that is going to make me a better man the next time I'm in a room with somebody else facing a crisis.

I maybe only will be one-hundreth of one-tenth of 1 percent better, but I'll be better. I'll be more empathetic. I'll be more understanding. I've seen something that I've never seen before. I heard things that I've never heard before. I listened to somebody articulate experiences that I could never imagine facing—and that's going to make me better for the next person that I talk to. That this lady chose to confide in me and ask my advice because she trusts me makes me feel both exalted and humbled. That's what I'm here on Earth for. That's the whole gig; that's why we run the kind of company we run, so people like her will feel, "This is just the best place in the world to work, because the people that work here are the best people they can possibly be." That she felt she could trust me means a lot to me now.

Would being considered worthy of her trust have meant a lot to me twenty-five years ago? Nope—I couldn't have cared less. All I wanted to do was win, win, win, and kick ass, kick ass, kick ass. I didn't get it. I got it more than a lot of other people did because of some of my life experiences, but I never focused on individuals as much as I have in the last five to ten years. And I like life better doing that.

See, that's the funny thing about this: Did I help her? I sure hope so. And if I did, pat me on the back, but I helped *me* as well. You can't beat that one-two punch. If you help somebody else and you help yourself, that's a pretty good use of an hour of your time.

I spend a lot less time screwing up than I used to. Do I screw up? Yep. Am I unapproachable sometimes? Yep. Am I insensitive sometimes? Yep. Do I get angry sometimes? Yep, although a fraction of the amount I used to. And so, guess what? I'm more productive.

And because productivity matters, guess what? I'm happier. And because I'm happier, I'm more productive. Isn't that a crazy circle?

It's not a secret. It's not a mojo. It's not a Ouija board. It's not a crystal ball. It's right there in your own head.

You're in charge.

You've got to tell yourself the truth.

You've got to find out why.

And you can do anything that you can visualize.

SERENITY PRAYER

—Reinhold Niebuhr (1892-1971)

God grant me the serenity

to accept the things I cannot change;

Courage to change the things I can;

and wisdom to know the difference.

THINK ABOUT IT:

Is what you say in alignment with what you do? Are you actively engaged in making yourself a better person, and making the world around you a better place? If not you, then who? If not now, when?

- **Choose happiness**: The quickest way to get there is to make others happy around you. Small acts of kindness make the world better, and make you feel better about yourself.

- **Take responsibility**: Don't be the person looking for a handout, or expecting others to give you what you need. If you're old enough to be reading this book, then you're old enough to take care of yourself. Get on with it.

- **Stop making excuses**: Nobody's life is free of pain, of conflict, or of failures. Everyone loses; everyone experiences reverses. Stop repeating the tired old script that you use to shrug off responsibility for your failures. Own them, and move forward. You'll travel lighter and faster without all that baggage to carry.

- **Take care of yourself**: Putting yourself first means that you'll have the energy and the resources you need to care for those who depend on you.

About RE/MAX Results

What do we do differently at RE/MAX Results? What's the secret sauce that's allowed us to experience the exponential growth we've enjoyed, and what drives us forward? I get asked that a lot. I think comes down to the philosophy that Bill and I brought to the enterprise when we started it up: *we know who the customer is.*

At RE/MAX Results, the sales executives are the customers. The buyers and sellers pay the sales executives, and *we* work for *them*, not the other way around. We empower our sales executives by providing superior customer service to those buyers and sellers, and by giving them the discretion to make business decisions on their own. It's a seemingly simple distinction that's had a surprisingly profound impact on our success.

If you'd like to know more about that business philosophy and how it can work for your enterprise, I'd be happy to hear from you.